Th

WHISKEY TASTING *Notebook*

Rye, Malt, Tennessee, and Others

(except Bourbon)

SUSAN REIGLER

—ᚙ—

MICHAEL VEACH

Acclaim Press

MORLEY, MISSOURI

Acclaim Press
— *Your Next Great Book* —

P.O. Box 238
Morley, MO 63767
(573) 472-9800
www.acclaimpress.com

Book & Cover Design: M. Frene Melton

ISBN: 978-1-948901-38-3 | 1-948901-38-2
Library of Congress Control Number: 2019947819

First Printing: 2019
Printed in the United States of America
10 9 8 7 6 5 4 3 2 1

CONTENTS

For Joanna
and
For Rosemary

PREFACE

Four years ago, we published the first edition of *The Bourbon Tasting Notebook*. A second edition came out last year with 50% more bourbons. Fingers crossed, the third edition—with well over 400 bourbons—will be out soon, if it has not already hit the shelves by the time you read this. Bourbon is still the undisputed leader of American whiskeys, and indeed, a truly native spirit, but other whiskey styles are gaining in popularity, too. This book will help you keep track of those as well.

Distillers across the country are trying their hands at ryes, malts, wheat whiskeys, and unusual grains. Because Tennessee whiskey, even though—like bourbon—is based on corn, it is made with an extra step of being filtered through sugar maple charcoal before put in barrels for aging. We didn't include Tennessee whiskey in the bourbon book. We include it here.

Of all the various non-bourbon types, rye is by far, the most prevalent. But malts are coming on strong. We tasted well over 200 whiskies for this book and we are certain that we will have many more than that for the next edition. That said, one reason for the diversity is that so many whiskeys are only available in a producer's home state, or available regionally. During the past year, when either of us travelled, we scouted for regional whiskeys. Friends brought us whiskey from their trips. (Thank you, Carol Ormay and Rosemary Miller.)

Once again, as they did for *The Bourbon Tasting Notebook*, the proprietors of Westport Whiskey & Wine in Louisville, Kentucky allowed us to raid their tasting room cabinet and sample whiskeys we did not own or of which we had not been sent samples. Many thanks to Chris Zaborowski and Richard Splan!

So, this book is designed for the whiskey curious, for individuals who wish to keep track of their tasting experiences. We encourage to have fun and, above all, to taste responsibly.

Cheers!
Susan & Mike

Nuts and Bolts

How to Use This Book

We wrote this whiskey tasting notebook so that you, the whiskey curious, will have a useful logbook for keeping track of your explorations. Unlike the authors of many other beverage tasting guides, we have not attempted to say which whiskeys are best or to assign ratings. As with our previous volume, *The Bourbon Tasting Notebook*, we are leaving that up to you. After all, taste is highly personal and subjective.

So, while there are no ratings, here is the information we include for the whiskeys:

Proof: Ranging from 80 proof to barrel proof.

Age: Fewer distillers are giving specific age information, but when stated on the label, we included it. If not, you'll see NAS for No Age Statement. If a whiskey is called "straight" you'll know it's at least two years old.

Type: Examples include bottled-in-bond, finished, extra aged (10 years or more), and so on.

Color: From lightest to darkest: Pale Straw, Light Straw, Straw, Dark Straw, Light Amber, Amber, Dark Amber, Bronze (straw have yellow hues; ambers contain reddish ones.) Often, but not always, the longer the whiskey has aged, the darker the color. Higher proof whiskies, or those finished in wine barrels, may be darker, too.

Price: Price scale is based on what you would pay for the whiskey in Kentucky or, if not made in Kentucky, its state of origin. In any case, the price is relative and subject to change. Prices may be higher in other markets.

$ = $15 and under
$$ = $16-$25
$$$ = $26-$35
$$$$ = $36-$55
$$$$$ = $56-$99
$$$$$$ = $100 and more

Mash Bill: When known, we include this.

Nose: We let the whiskeys warm in Glencairn tasting glasses before nosing to detect characteristic aromas. To buy your own Glencairn glasses, go to a local liquor store or www.whiskyglass.com. You can also use any tulip shaped glass, such as a white wine or sherry glass, or a snifter.

Taste: Descriptors include flavors such as fruits, nuts, spices, sweets, and herbs. We also note mouthfeel. We usually sipped without water, but we sometimes added a few drops of water to higher proof bourbons, especially those bottled at barrel proof.

Finish: The flavors revealed on the palate after the bourbon has been swallowed.

Notes: The distiller or producer and our general comments about the whiskey, which may include overall impressions, suggestions for enjoyment, and other information.

Again, we have not assigned numerical ratings to the whiskeys. We are leaving that to you, since only you know which whiskeys you like and for what reasons. Space is provided for your notes and ratings for each.

The book is arranged by whiskey styles, which are alphabetical, beginning with "American Whiskeys" and ending with "Wheat Whiskeys." Here's how to know which is which.

American Whiskeys

Bourbon is, of course, just one style of American whiskey. The Federal agency, the Alcohol and Tobacco Tax and Trade Bureau (TTB) has set the standards of identity for all alcoholic beverages sold in the United States. You can find this on the Internet at **www.ttb.gov**. But we quote the ones about the whiskeys in this book to lay the ground rules:

The Standards of Identity for Whisky

Class 2: Whisky. "Whisky" is an alcoholic distillate from a fermented mash of grain produced at less than 190 proof in such a manner that the distillate possesses the taste, aroma, and characteristics generally attributed to whisky, stored in oak containers (except that of corn whisky need not be so stored), and bottled at not less than 80 proof, and also includes mixtures of such distillates for which no specific standards of identity are prescribed.

This is the rule to simply be a whiskey. It is recognized by the international market as the definition of whisky.

The standards of identity go further to describe the categories of American whisky. Under this definition there are several rules for the categories being looked at in this book. They are as follows:

(i) "Bourbon whisky", "rye whisky", "wheat whisky", "malt whisky", or "rye malt" whisky" is whisky produced at not exceeding 160 proof from a fermented mash of nor less than 51% corn, rye, malted barley, or malted rye grain, respectively, and stored at not more than 125 proof in charred new oak containers; and also includes mixtures of such whiskies of the same type.

(ii) "Corn whisky" is whiskey produced at not exceeding 160 proof from a fermented mash of not less than 80% corn grain, and if stored in oak containers stored at not more than 125 proof in used or uncharred new oak containers and not subjected in any manner to treatment with charred wood; and also includes mixtures of such whiskey.

(iii) Whiskies conforming to the standards prescribed in paragraphs (b) (1) (i) and (ii) of this section, which have been stored in the type of oak containers prescribed, for a period of 2 years or more shall be further designated as "straight"; for example, "straight bourbon whisky", "straight corn whisky" and whisky conforming to the standards prescribed in paragraph (b) (1) (i) of this section except that it was produced from a mash of less than 51 percent of any type of grain, and stored for a period of 2 years or more in charred new oak containers shall be designated merely as "straight whisky" includes mixtures of straight whiskies of the same type produced in the same State.

2. "Whisky distilled from bourbon (rye, wheat, malt, or rye) mash" is a whiskey produced in the United States at not exceeding 160 proof from a fermented mash of not less than 51 percent corn, rye, wheat, malted barley, or malted rye grain, respectively, and stored in used oak containers; and also includes mixtures of such whiskies of the same type. Whisky conforming to the standard of identity for corn whisky must be designated corn whisky.

3. "Light whisky" is whisky produced in the United States at more than 160 proof, on or after January 26, 1968, and stored in used or uncharred new oak containers; and also includes mixtures of such whiskies. If "light whisky" is mixed with less than 20 percent of straight whisky on a proof gallon basis, the mixture shall be designated "blended light whisky" (light whisky – a blend).

4. "Blended whisky" (whisky – a blend) is a mixture which contains straight whisky or a blend of straight whiskies at not less than 20 percent on a proof gallon basis, excluding alcohol derived from harmless coloring, flavoring or blending materials, and, separately, or in combination, whisky or neutral spirits. A blended whisky containing not less than 51 percent on a proof gallon basis of one of the types of straight whisky shall be further designated by the specific type of straight whisky; for example, "blended rye whisky" (rye whisky – a blend).

5. (i) "A blend of straight whiskies" (blended straight whiskies) is a mixture of straight whiskies which does not conform to the standard of identity for "straight whisky". Products so designated may contain harmless coloring, flavoring or blending materials.

(ii) "A blend of straight whiskies" (blended straight whiskies) consisting entirely of one of the types of straight whisky, and not conforming to the standard for straight whiskey, shall be further designated by that type of straight whisky; for example, "a blend of straight rye whiskies" (blended straight rye whiskies). "A blend of straight whiskies" consisting entirely of one of the types of straight whisky shall include straight whisky of the same type which was produced in the same State or by the same proprietor within the same State, provided that such whisky contains harmless coloring, flavoring or blending materials as stated in 27 CFR 5.23 (a).

(iii) The harmless coloring, flavoring, or blending materials allowed under this section shall not include neutral spirits or alcohol in their original state. Neutral spirits or alcohol may only appear in a "blend of straight whiskies" or in a "blend of straight whiskies consisting of one of the types of straight whisky" as a vehicle for recognized flavoring of blending material.

The Indices

Finally, we include several different idicies at the end of the book to help you find particular whiskeys and to help you organize your tastings. In addition to an alphabetical index of all brands (there are more than 200 in the book); we have also listed them by Proof, Price, Special Style, and State.

Chapter One
American Whiskey

American whiskey is a catchall category for whiskeys that don't fall into one of the categories of the standards of identity. This could be for several reasons: the mash bill may not have a dominant grain, the distiller blended different types of whiskey together to create the brand, or they may have used cooperage more than once in the aging process. There is a tradition of this type of whiskey going back to the 19th century before there were standards of identity to conform to, and this whiskey was often labeled as "Bourbon" or "rye". With the introduction of the standards in the 20th century, the category of "American Whiskey" was born.

David James Straight American Whiskey

Proof:	119.6
Age:	10 years
Type:	Straight
Style:	American Whiskey
Mash Bill:	Not disclosed
Color:	Pale Straw
Price:	$$$$$

Mike
Nose: Vanilla, with a hint of maple syrup and apples.
Taste: Vanilla, with maple syrup on pancakes with a hint of baking spices.
Finish: Long and spicy.

Susan
Nose: Brown sugar, vanilla, and faint, sweet fruit.
Taste: Baked pineapple with brown sugar, some vanilla.
Finish: Pepper drying to oak.

Notes
Sourced from Indiana for Old Georgetown Spirits Company, Georgetown, KY.

My Score

Notes: _____

_____

_____

Appearance (1-5)	____	Nose (1-25)	____
Taste (1-25)	____	Finish (1-25)	____
Complexity (1-10)	____	Overall Impression (1-10)	____

SCORE ____

Early Times Kentucky Whiskey

Proof:	80
Age:	At least 3 years
Type:	Not straight
Style:	American Whiskey
Mash Bill:	79% corn, 11% rye, 10% malted barley
Color:	Very Pale Straw
Price:	$

Mike

Nose: Vanilla and corn with just a hint of oak.
Taste: Vanilla and corn with a hint of pepper spice.
Finish: Medium long and peppery.

Susan

Nose: Corn and oak with a whisper of fruit.
Taste: Frosted corn flakes with some cherries and caramel, plus a dash of bitter chocolate.
Finish: Warm, drying to black pepper.

Notes

Aged in used cooperage. Brown-Forman Distillery, Louisville, Kentucky, which also makes a bourbon expression and a bonded bourbon expression with this mash bill and strain of yeast. Far more flavorful than the color would suggest and a great bargain sip.

My Score	
Notes: _____	
_____	
_____	
Appearance (1-5) ____	Nose (1-25) ____
Taste (1-25) ____	Finish (1-25) ____
Complexity (1-10) ____	Overall Impression (1-10) ____
SCORE ____	

The Gentleman American Whiskey

Proof: 100
Age: NAS
Type: Not straight
Style: American Whiskey
Mash Bill: 62% corn, 28% rye, 10% barley
Color: Straw
Price: $$$ (375 mL)

Mike

Nose: Young whiskey. Apricots or peaches with a hint of oak.
Taste: Very thin. Corn, vanilla, with a hint of oak.
Finish: Long and oaky.

Susan

Nose: Dominated by grain with some tobacco and pepper.
Taste: Thin and grainy. Much drier than the nose.
Finish: Pipe bowl dottle.

Notes

Hartfield & Co., Paris, Kentucky. Aged in ex-bourbon barrels.

My Score

Notes: _____

_____

_____

Appearance (1-5) ____   Nose (1-25) ____
Taste (1-25) ____   Finish (1-25) ____
Complexity (1-10) ____   Overall Impression (1-10) ____
SCORE ____

Geyser Distilling Whiskey

Proof:	90
Age:	NAS
Type:	Not straight
Style:	American Whiskey
Mash Bill:	Includes corn
Color:	Very Pale Straw
Price:	$$$$

Mike
Nose: Young. Grain, yeast and a hint of vanilla.
Taste: Very young. A little corn, vanilla, and pepper.
Finish: Short and peppery.

Susan
Nose: Corn, sweet mint, white pepper. Yeasty. Very young.
Taste: Raw corn with whispers of apple/pear and cinnamon.
Finish: Pepper drying to oak.

Notes
Glacier Distilling, Cody, Wyoming. Proofed with water from Yellowstone National Park. Did we mention it tastes young? Would be very interested to try this when it has some age on it.

My Score

Notes: _____

_____

_____

Appearance (1-5)	____	Nose (1-25)	____
Taste (1-25)	____	Finish (1-25)	____
Complexity (1-10)	____	Overall Impression (1-10)	____

SCORE ____

James Oliver American Whiskey

Proof:	86
Age:	NAS
Type:	Finished
Style:	American Whiskey
Mash Bill:	High Rye
Color:	Straw
Price:	$$$

Mike

Nose: Corn, vanilla and a hint of citrus.

Taste: Corn, vanilla, a little orange zest and spice.

Finish: Long and spicy with a hint of oak.

Susan

Nose: Caramel, grapefruit, and a touch of rye spice.

Taste: Dark fruit, like dates and raisins, with some baked apple and vanilla.

Finish: Long and spicy with oak.

Notes

Indio Spirits, Portland, Oregon. First aged in ex-bourbon barrels and then finished in ex-sherry barrels.

My Score

Notes: _____

_____

_____

Appearance (1-5)	____	Nose (1-25)	____
Taste (1-25)	____	Finish (1-25)	____
Complexity (1-10)	____	Overall Impression (1-10)	____

SCORE ____

Kings County Distillery Whiskey

Proof:	90
Age:	1 year or more
Type:	Not straight
Style:	American Whiskey
Mash Bill:	Not released
Color:	Light Amber
Price:	$$$$ (375 mL)

Mike

Nose: Very sweet. Vanilla and fruit, (berries?) with fine leather and tobacco.

Taste: Vanilla and berries with maybe a little pear and some baking spices and oak.

Finish: Ling and dry with oak and baking spices.

Susan

Nose: Toffee, tobacco, and cereal.

Taste: Multigrain cereal with a smattering of dried apricots and a dash of cinnamon.

Finish: Very dry and spicy.

Notes

Kings County Distillery, Brooklyn, New York. Is this "American whiskey" because no portion of grain reaches 50%? Distillery located in historic red brick gatehouse on the grounds of the Brooklyn Navy Yard.

My Score

Notes: _____

_____

_____

Appearance (1-5)	____	Nose (1-25)	____
Taste (1-25)	____	Finish (1-25)	____
Complexity (1-10)	____	Overall Impression (1-10)	____

SCORE ____

Koval Four Grain

Proof:	94
Age:	NAS
Type:	Single Barrel
Style:	American Whiskey
Mash Bill:	Rye, malted barley, oats, wheat
Color:	Pale Straw
Price:	$$$$

Mike

Nose: Plums and apricots with a little cereal grain.

Taste: Fruity. Plums, apricots, and peaches with vanilla and a little pepper and oak.

Finish: Long and spicy with oak and pepper.

Susan

Nose: Cellulose tape, vanilla, pears.

Taste: Vanilla with pears and some cinnamon.

Finish: A bit of oak with lingering fruit.

Notes

Koval Distillery, Chicago, Illinois. Barrel 310. All grains organically grown.

My Score

Notes: _____

_____

_____

Appearance (1-5) _____   Nose (1-25) _____

Taste (1-25) _____   Finish (1-25) _____

Complexity (1-10) _____   Overall Impression (1-10) _____

SCORE _____

MB Roland Dark Fired Whiskey

Proof:	114.4
Age:	NAS
Type:	Barrel Strength
Style:	American Whiskey
Mash Bill:	45% white corn, 17% rye, 33% dark fired corn, 5% malted barley
Color:	Barely tinted
Price:	$$$$

Mike
Nose: Corn and smoke, but not too much smoke. A hint of fruit and spice.
Taste: Corn, smoke, vanilla, and a little pear and peach. Lots of pepper.
Finish: Long with smoke and pepper.

Susan
Nose: Grilled corn on the cob, wood smoke, spices.
Taste: Mouthful of campfire, then sweet vanilla with pears, corn, and oak.
Finish: Sweetness lingers on the tongue to merge with pepper and oak.

Notes
MB Roland Distillery, Pembroke, KY. Aged in ex-bourbon barrels. Batch 27, barrel 37 of 181. Distillery has a small building where it smokes grain.

My Score

Notes: _____

_____

_____

Appearance (1-5) _____   Nose (1-25) _____

Taste (1-25) _____   Finish (1-25) _____

Complexity (1-10) _____   Overall Impression (1-10) _____

SCORE _____

Michter's US★1 Unblended Small Batch American Whiskey

Proof:	83.4
Age:	NAS
Type:	Small Batch
Style:	American Whiskey
Mash Bill:	Not disclosed
Color:	Pale Straw
Price:	$$$$

Mike
Nose: Caramel, vanilla, corn, and a hint of oak.
Taste: Buttered caramel, fruit – berries and pears – with some baking spices.
Finish: Starts sweet with vanilla and fruit, but dries out with some oak tannins.

Susan
Nose: Light corn and apples with some buttered popcorn.
Taste: Sweet vanilla, apples, sweet spice.
Finish: Lingering and smooth with vanilla and sweet oak.

Notes
Michter's Distillery, Louisville, Kentucky. Since this is aged in used cooperage, it does not qualify as bourbon.

My Score

Notes: _____

_____

_____

Appearance (1-5) ____   Nose (1-25) ____

Taste (1-25) ____   Finish (1-25) ____

Complexity (1-10) ____   Overall Impression (1-10) ____

SCORE ____

Michter's US★1 Sour Mash Whiskey

Proof:	86
Age:	NAS
Type:	Small Batch
Style:	American Whiskey
Mash Bill:	Not disclosed
Color:	Pale Straw
Price:	$$$$

Mike

Nose: Rich caramel, baking spices, and a hint of chocolate.

Taste: Caramel, apples, baking spices – nutmeg and cinnamon – and a bit of oak.

Finish: Long and dry with oak and spice.

Susan

Nose: Crème brulee and sweet spice with toffee top notes.

Taste: Caramel nougat with some banana.

Finish: Peppery and lingering.

Notes

Michter's Distillery, Louisville, Kentucky. The original mash bill was 45% rye, 45% corn, 10% malted barley, but changed after the brand was acquired by Chatham Brands. Can't be too changed, since this is unblended and not enough of any one grain to qualify as bourbon or rye.

My Score

Notes: _____

_____

_____

Appearance (1-5) ____   Nose (1-25) ____

Taste (1-25) ____   Finish (1-25) ____

Complexity (1-10) ____   Overall Impression (1-10) ____

SCORE ____

Palmetto Whiskey

Proof:	89.3
Age:	NAS
Type:	Not straight
Style:	American Whiskey
Mash Bill:	21% rye, plus corn, malted barley, and wheat
Color:	Pale Straw
Price:	$$$

Mike

Nose: Floor wax and oak.

Taste: Rotten fruit, oak, and little pepper and oak.

Finish: Short, but too long with oak and rotten fruit.

Susan

Nose: Unusual. Cooking rice? Some light apple.

Taste: Very simple. Almost like mineral water with a bit of spice.

Finish: Disappears quickly.

Notes

Palmetto Distilling, Anderson, South Carolina.

My Score

Notes: _____

_____

_____

Appearance (1-5) _____   Nose (1-25) _____

Taste (1-25) _____   Finish (1-25) _____

Complexity (1-10) _____   Overall Impression (1-10) _____

SCORE _____

Ransom The Emerald 1865

Proof:	87.6
Age:	3 years
Type:	Irish Mash Bill
Style:	American Whiskey
Mash Bill:	Barley
Color:	Straw
Price:	$$$$$

Mike

Nose: Very grain forward with a little vanilla and chocolate.

Taste: Vanilla, with a hint of milk chocolate, pepper, and oak.

Finish: Very short with chocolate notes and oak.

Susan

Nose: Malt, apples, some vanilla and caramel, plus more cereal grains.

Taste: Malt and Apples with oak and pepper.

Finish: Very dry and oaky.

Notes

Ransom Wine Co. & Distillery, McMinnville, Oregon. Models on an Irish whiskey mash bill form 1865. Made in alembic pot still and aged in French and American oak.

My Score

Notes: _____

_____

_____

Appearance (1-5) _____   Nose (1-25) _____

Taste (1-25) _____   Finish (1-25) _____

Complexity (1-10) _____   Overall Impression (1-10) _____

SCORE _____

Rebel Yell American Whiskey

Proof:	90
Age:	24 months
Type:	Small Batch
Style:	American
Mash Bill:	Mingling of bourbon and rye whiskeys
Color:	Pale Straw
Price:	$$

Mike

Nose:	Rye grass, corn, vanilla, and a hint of spice.
Taste:	Rye grass, vanilla, with a hint of citrus.
Finish:	Long and grassy with a hint of oak.

Susan

Nose:	Vanilla custard with a sprinkling of nutmeg and a little bit of ripe apple.
Taste:	Fruit up front, with some herbal rye following. Not complex.
Finish:	Dry and grassy. Some oak.

Notes

Luxco, St. Louis, Missouri. Whiskeys currently sourced, but Luxco now has a distillery, Lux Row, in Bardstown, Kentucky.

My Score

Notes: _____

_____

_____

Appearance (1-5)	____	Nose (1-25)	____
Taste (1-25)	____	Finish (1-25)	____
Complexity (1-10)	____	Overall Impression (1-10)	____

SCORE ____

Sam Houston American Whiskey

Proof:	86
Age:	NAS
Type:	Straight
Style:	American Whiskey
Mash Bill:	Not released
Color:	Pale Straw
Price:	$$

Mike

Nose: Corn, vanilla, leather, oak.
Taste: Vanilla, a little fruit, and lots of pepper spice.
Finish: Long and spicy.

Susan

Nose: Herbal with some underlying leather and brown sugar.
Taste: Cornflakes, cinnamon, some tobacco and vanilla.
Finish: Warm with smoke.

Notes

Bottled by Western Spirits, Bowling Green, Kentucky.

My Score

Notes: _____

_____

_____

Appearance (1-5) ____   Nose (1-25) ____

Taste (1-25) ____   Finish (1-25) ____

Complexity (1-10) ____   Overall Impression (1-10) ____

SCORE ____

Second Glance American Whiskey

Proof:	88
Age:	NAS
Type:	Not straight
Style:	American Whiskey
Mash Bill:	95% corn, 4% rye, 1% malted barley
Color:	Very Pale Straw
Price:	$$$$

Mike
Nose:	Very fruity. Banana or pineapple (?) with a hint of herbs.
Taste:	Corn, vanilla, and a little oak and spice.
Finish:	Medium long and tannic.

Susan
Nose:	Sweet mint, orange-pineapple juice.
Taste:	More sweet mint and some vanilla.
Finish:	Starts sweet before changing to a very dry finish. But not spicy.

Notes
Sourced Kentucky bourbons mingled and bottled by Savage & Cooke, American Canyon, California. Youngest whiskey in the bottling is 5 years old.

My Score

Notes: _____

_____

_____

Appearance (1-5)	____	Nose (1-25) ____
Taste (1-25)	____	Finish (1-25) ____
Complexity (1-10)	____	Overall Impression (1-10) ____

SCORE ____

Shenk's Sour Mash

Proof:	91.2
Age:	NAS
Type:	Sour Mash
Style:	American Whiskey
Mash Bill:	Not disclosed
Color:	Straw
Price:	$$$$$$

Mike
Nose:	Butterscotch, apples, and oak.
Taste:	Butterscotch, apples, oak, and a hint of pepper.
Finish:	Long with oak and spice and a hint of butterscotch.

Susan
Nose:	Honey, apples, vanilla, and light spice.
Taste:	Caramel, vanilla, light cheery fruit with new leather and brown sugar.
Finish:	Spicy with a little butterscotch and oak.

Notes
Michter's Distillery, Louisville, Kentucky. Bottle 2393 of batch 18C321, 2018 release. Limited annual release from Michter's.

My Score

Notes: _____

_____

_____

Appearance (1-5)	____	Nose (1-25)	____
Taste (1-25)	____	Finish (1-25)	____
Complexity (1-10)	____	Overall Impression (1-10)	____

SCORE ____

Additional American Whiskey Releases

Name: _____

Distillery: _____

Proof: _____   **Mash Bill:** _____
Age: _____   _____
Type: _____   **Color:** _____
Style: _____   **Price:** _____

My Score

Notes: _____
_____
_____

Appearance (1-5) _____   Nose (1-25) _____
Taste (1-25) _____   Finish (1-25) _____
Complexity (1-10) _____   Overall Impression (1-10) _____
SCORE _____

Name: _____

Distillery: _____

Proof: _____   **Mash Bill:** _____
Age: _____   _____
Type: _____   **Color:** _____
Style: _____   **Price:** _____

My Score

Notes: _____
_____
_____

Appearance (1-5) _____   Nose (1-25) _____
Taste (1-25) _____   Finish (1-25) _____
Complexity (1-10) _____   Overall Impression (1-10) _____
SCORE _____

Chapter Two
Blended Whiskey

Blended whiskey dates back to the 19th century. The idea of adding alcohol in its unaged form to aged whiskey was an inexpensive way to produce a lot of whiskey. It was not until the Taft Decision on Whisky was published on 27 December 1909 that such whiskey had to be labeled as blended whiskey. The other important part of the Taft Decision was that such whiskeys had to have grain neutral spirits and not neutral spirits made from other sources such as fruits or cane sugar. Today, blended whiskey is a small category in the United States.

Alibi American Blended Whiskey

Proof:	90
Age:	NAS
Type:	Not straight
Style:	Blend
Mash Bill:	27.5% straight whiskey, 72.5% grain neutral spirits
Color:	Very, Very Pale Straw
Price:	$$

Mike
Nose: Neutral spirits, corn, vanilla, and a hint of oak.
Taste: Very light. A little berry fruit, vanilla, and oak.
Finish: Short and sweet with berry fruit

Susan
Nose: Bourbon-esque nose of caramel corn and some honey.
Taste: Sweet corn, light honey, and floral notes, with some peaches.
Finish: Peaches linger.

Notes
Blended and bottled by Alibi American Whiskey, Auburndale, Florida. Label states that the whiskeys used were at least three years old.

My Score

Notes: _____

_____

_____

Appearance (1-5) ____   Nose (1-25) ____

Taste (1-25) ____   Finish (1-25) ____

Complexity (1-10) ____   Overall Impression (1-10) ____

SCORE ____

Calvert Extra

Proof:	80
Age:	NAS
Type:	Not straight
Style:	Blended
Mash Bill:	30% straight whiskey 70% grain neutral spirits
Color:	Almost none
Price:	$

Mike

Nose: Very light vanilla with a hint of fruit.

Taste: Very thin, with vanilla, berries – strawberry and raspberry – with a hint of oak.

Finish: Short with some wood tannins.

Susan

Nose: Corn and alcohol. Very light.

Taste: Frosted corn flakes with a suggestion of vanilla and apple.

Finish: Vanilla actually lingers for a bit.

Notes

Jim Beam Distillery, Clermont, Kentucky. Add ice and you'll have your "lawnmower whiskey."

My Score

Notes: _____

_____

_____

Appearance (1-5) ____   Nose (1-25) ____

Taste (1-25) ____   Finish (1-25) ____

Complexity (1-10) ____   Overall Impression (1-10) ____

SCORE ____

Crooked Furrow Harvest Blend

Proof:	88.4
Age:	2 years
Type:	Non-Chill Filtered
Style:	Blended
Mash Bill:	60% straight whiskey
	40% grain neutral spirits
Color:	Pale Straw
Price:	$$$$

Mike

Nose: Young whiskey and neutral spirits with a little corn and vanilla.

Taste: Caramel, vanilla, and a hint of oak.

Finish: Short with only a little oak and pepper spice.

Susan

Nose: Corn, some ripe apple, but very light.

Taste: Roasted corn, some fruit, some oak.

Finish: Short and peppery.

Notes

Proof Artisan Distiller, Fargo, North Dakota. Not offensive.

My Score

Notes: _____

_____

_____

Appearance (1-5)	____	Nose (1-25)	____
Taste (1-25)	____	Finish (1-25)	____
Complexity (1-10)	____	Overall Impression (1-10)	____

SCORE ____

Henderson Blended American Whiskey

Proof:	80
Age:	NAS
Type:	Not straight
Style:	Blended
Mash Bill:	At least 20% straight whiskey
Color:	Slightly tinted
Price:	$

Mike

Nose: Corn, banana, and a hint of vanilla.

Taste: Thin and watery – very little flavor. Hint of vanilla.

Finish: Short, with only a hint of oak.

Susan

Nose: Some spice and dark fruit and a tiny touch of burnt caramel.

Taste: Some faint caramel and pepper.

Finish: Very warm for 80 proof. Leaves lips tingling.

Notes

Bottled by Henderson, Dallas, Texas.

My Score

Notes: _____

_____

_____

Appearance (1-5)	____	Nose (1-25)	____
Taste (1-25)	____	Finish (1-25)	____
Complexity (1-10)	____	Overall Impression (1-10)	____

SCORE ____

Kessler

Proof:	80
Age:	Whiskeys at least 2 years
Type:	Not straight
Style:	Blended
Mash Bill:	72.5% grain neutral spirits, 27.5% straight whiskeys
Color:	Very Pale Straw
Price:	$

Mike

Nose: Very light. Vanilla and corn with a hint – just a hint – of fruit.

Taste: Vanilla and corn with a hint of apples.

Finish: Short, but dry, with oak.

Susan

Nose: Extremely light. Some corn sweetness.

Taste: Ripe apples and candy corn, but faint.

Finish: Short and warm.

Notes

Jim Beam Distillery, Clermont, Kentucky.

My Score

Notes: _____

_____

_____

Appearance (1-5) _____   Nose (1-25) _____

Taste (1-25) _____   Finish (1-25) _____

Complexity (1-10) _____   Overall Impression (1-10) _____

SCORE _____

Seagram's 7 Crown

Proof:	80
Age:	NAS
Type:	Not straight
Style:	Blended
Mash Bill:	At least 20% straight whiskey
Color:	Slightly tinted
Price:	$

Mike

Nose: Corn, banana, and a hint of vanilla.

Taste: Thin and watery – very little flavor. Hint of vanilla.

Finish: Short, with only a hint of oak.

Susan

Nose: Some spice and dark fruit and a tiny touch of burnt caramel.

Taste: Some faint caramel and pepper.

Finish: Very warm for 80 proof. Leaves lips tingling.

Notes

Bottled by Henderson, Dallas, Texas.

My Score

Notes: _____

_____

_____

Appearance (1-5) _____   Nose (1-25) _____

Taste (1-25) _____   Finish (1-25) _____

Complexity (1-10) _____   Overall Impression (1-10) _____

SCORE _____

Additional Blended Whiskey Releases

Name: _____

Distillery: _____

Proof: _____ **Mash Bill:** _____
Age: _____ _____
Type: _____ **Color:** _____
Style: _____ **Price:** _____

My Score

Notes: _____

_____

_____

Appearance (1-5) _____ Nose (1-25) _____
Taste (1-25) _____ Finish (1-25) _____
Complexity (1-10) _____ Overall Impression (1-10) _____

SCORE _____

Name: _____

Distillery: _____

Proof: _____ **Mash Bill:** _____
Age: _____ _____
Type: _____ **Color:** _____
Style: _____ **Price:** _____

My Score

Notes: _____

_____

_____

Appearance (1-5) _____ Nose (1-25) _____
Taste (1-25) _____ Finish (1-25) _____
Complexity (1-10) _____ Overall Impression (1-10) _____

SCORE _____

CHAPTER THREE
BLENDS

This is different from "blended" in that no grain neutral spirits are added. Distillers are mingling various whiskies to get a flavor profile, a practice that has been traditional in Scotland and recently gained in popularity in the U.S. These include blends of different types of whiskey, such as bourbon and rye, and even whiskies sourced from other countries.

Amador Ten Barrels Straight Hop-Flavored Whiskey

Proof:	96
Age:	See comments
Type:	Straight, Finished
Style:	Blend
Mash Bill:	Includes 2-row barley
Color:	Straw
Price:	$$$$$$

Mike

Nose:	Grapefruit and vanilla with a hint of chocolate.
Taste:	Grapefruit, chocolate, vanilla and a hint of pepper.
Finish:	Medium long and fruity.

Susan

Nose:	Hoppy bitterness with citrus, wood, and spice.
Taste:	Caramel, grapefruit, hops, and some vanilla.
Finish:	Smoke at the beginning drying to intense oak.

Notes

Amador Whiskey Co., St. Helena, California. Batch 1, Bottle 2206. Sourced malt whiskey aged and whiskey distilled from Bear Republic IPA. (Hence that grapefruity note. Bet Cascade hops were used.) Aged for two years in French oak wine barrels and two years in chardonnay barrels.

My Score		
Notes: _____		
_____		
_____		
Appearance (1-5) _____	Nose (1-25)	_____
Taste (1-25) _____	Finish (1-25)	_____
Complexity (1-10) _____	Overall Impression (1-10)	_____
SCORE _____		

Barrell Dovetail

Proof:	122.9
Age:	10 years
Type:	Finished, Barrel Strength
Style:	Blend
Mash Bill:	See comments
Color:	Light Straw
Price:	$$$$$

Mike

Nose:	Molasses, some berries and oak. Molasses overpowers the other aromas.
Taste:	Molasses, raspberries, blackberries and lots of white pepper spice with a hint of oak.
Finish:	Surprisingly short, but spicy.

Susan

Nose:	Sweet wine notes jump out first followed by burnt toffee and rye spice.
Taste:	Wine with some whisky notes. Naturally a bit hot at this proof. Water reveals berry fruit and vanilla.
Finish:	Short and peppery.

Notes

Sourced and blended by Barrell Craft Spirits, Louisville, Kentucky. Contains 10-year-old Indiana whiskey and 11-year-old Tennessee bourbon. They were finished in rum, port, and Dunn Vineyards cabernet barrels.

My Score

Notes: _____

_____

_____

Appearance (1-5) ____	Nose (1-25)	____
Taste (1-25) ____	Finish (1-25)	____
Complexity (1-10) ____	Overall Impression (1-10) ____
SCORE ____		

Barrell Whiskey Infinate Barrell Project

Proof:	119.3
Age:	Bottled 9 May 2018 – see below
Type:	Barrel Strength
Style:	Blend
Mash Bill:	See comments
Color:	Pale Straw
Price:	$$$$$

Mike

Nose: Malt, fruit, oak, sawdust.

Taste: Malt, corn, rye grass, vanilla, and a hint of pepper. Some fruit – berries and apples – in the background.

Finish: Very dry and spicy with pepper oak.

Susan

Nose: Fruit and spice, but quite a hodgepodge. Citrus emerges as it sits.

Taste: A little chocolaty, with some cinnamon and malted milk. Water releases fruit and stick candy.

Finish: Lingering. It is both sweet and spicy, before drying.

Notes

Sourced and blended by Barrell Craft Spirits, Louisville, Kentucky. Go to the web site, https://www.barrellbourbon.com/infinite, and find the bottling by date to see what whiskeys are in the blend. Water did not change this one for Mike. Very drinkable at this proof.

My Score

Notes: _____

_____

_____

Appearance (1-5)	_____	Nose (1-25)	_____
Taste (1-25)	_____	Finish (1-25)	_____
Complexity (1-10)	_____	Overall Impression (1-10)	_____

SCORE _____

Barrell Whiskey Infinate Barrell

Proof:	116.44
Age:	Bottled 16 July 2018 – see below
Type:	Barrel Strength
Style:	Blend
Mash Bill:	See comments
Color:	Pale Straw
Price:	$$$$$

Mike

Nose: Vanilla, cherries, and dates with a little oak spice.

Taste: Vanilla and cherries, dates and ripe apple with cinnamon spice and oak.

Finish: Medium long and dry with oak and spice.

Susan

Nose: Mint and malt with some rye grass.

Taste: Minty and spicy. Different fruit layers reveal themselves as the whiskey moves along the palate. Water brings out caramel.

Finish: Long, dry, and peppery.

Notes

Sourced and blended by Barrell Craft Spirits, Louisville, Kentucky. Web site explains, "selecting barrels for their flavor contribution and complexity and blending them in a larger single, or "Infinite" vessel. At each bottling we'll remove a portion of that whiskey and replace it with other barrels that will complement the remaining blend. You can find which whiskeys are present in each bottling by referring to the bottling date on the front label and going to that page on our site.

My Score		
Notes: _____		
_____		
_____		
Appearance (1-5) ____	Nose (1-25)	____
Taste (1-25) ____	Finish (1-25)	____
Complexity (1-10) ____	Overall Impression (1-10)	____
SCORE ____		

Bourye

Proof:	92
Age:	Minimum 10 years
Type:	Not straight
Style:	Blend
Mash Bill:	See comments
Color:	Straw
Price:	$$$$$

Mike

Nose: Very fruity with ripe plums and grapes, vanilla and a hint of baking spice.

Taste: Very thin and watery. Some sweet fruit – grapes.

Finish: Medium long and dry with oak and a hint of nutmeg.

Susan

Nose: Brown sugar, rye grass, caramel and a bit of ripe apple.

Taste: Initial mingling of caramel sweetness (bourbon) with spice from the rye. Only a little fruit.

Finish: Dry, but not spicy.

Notes

Sourced and blended High West Distillery, Park City, Utah. Blend of two MGP Lawrenceburg, Indiana, bourbons (75% corn, 21% rye, 4% malted barley and 60% corn, 36% rye, 4% malted barley) and one rye (95% rye, 5% malted barley). The jackalope on the label symbolizes this hybrid.

My Score

Notes: _____

_____

_____

Appearance (1-5)	____	Nose (1-25)	____
Taste (1-25)	____	Finish (1-25)	____
Complexity (1-10)	____	Overall Impression (1-10)	____
	SCORE ____		

Campfire

Proof:	92
Age:	NAS
Type:	Peated
Style:	Blend
Mash Bill:	Not disclosed
Color:	Light Straw
Price:	$$$$$

Mike

Nose: Smoky peat, vanilla, fruit (banana or cantalope?), and oak.

Taste: Smoky peat, vanilla, buttered toffee, and definitely cantalope, with a little pepper and oak.

Finish: Smoky with oak, peat, pepper, and a hint of toffee.

Susan

Nose: Vanilla, light smoke, with some leather and subtle berries.

Taste: Malted barley note predominates, followed by some corn and some smoke, with fruit and nuts.

Finish: Very dry and herbal with oak. Water bring out more fruit.

Notes

High West Distillery, Park City, Utah. Blend of bourbon, rye and peated Scotch whiskeys, 4-8 years old.

My Score

Notes: _____

_____

_____

Appearance (1-5) ____   Nose (1-25) ____

Taste (1-25) ____   Finish (1-25) ____

Complexity (1-10) ____   Overall Impression (1-10) ____

SCORE ____

Chicken Cock Bootlegger's Reserve

Proof:	90
Age:	6 months
Type:	Not straight
Style:	Blend
Mash Bill:	Blend of bourbon and rye whiskeys
Color:	Pale Straw
Price:	$$$$

Mike

Nose: Corn, vanilla, rye grass, and a hint of apricots.

Taste: Very young. Corn, rye grass, that hint of fruit, and vanilla.

Finish: Long and spicy with white pepper and oak.

Susan

Nose: Roasted corn, rye spice, and a little sweet mint.

Taste: Corn and apples with pepper and some sweet oak.

Finish: Dry and spicy. Stays spicy on the tongue for quite some time.

Notes

Chicken Cock Distillery Co., N. Charleston, South Carolina.

My Score

Notes: _____

_____

_____

Appearance (1-5) _____   Nose (1-25) _____

Taste (1-25) _____   Finish (1-25) _____

Complexity (1-10) _____   Overall Impression (1-10) _____

SCORE _____

Johnny Smoking Gun Whiskey

Proof:	87
Age:	NAS
Type:	Infused
Style:	Blend
Mash Bill:	70% 7-year corn whiskey, 30% young rye
Color:	Straw
Price:	$$$$

Mike

Nose: Smoke with some vanilla and apricots.

Taste: Smoke, apricots, vanilla, and a little baking spice.

Finish: Long, dry, with oak, spice and a hint of chocolate.

Susan

Nose: Grain forward with a bit of smoke followed by caraway seeds.

Taste: Smoked oysters with some chutney. Very different!

Finish: Long and dry.

Notes

Two James Spirits, Detroit, Michigan. Infused with a two-stage maceration of a proprietary blend of three Asian teas. Developed to complement Asian cuisine and it very well might.

My Score

Notes: _____

_____

_____

Appearance (1-5) ____   Nose (1-25) ____

Taste (1-25) ____   Finish (1-25) ____

Complexity (1-10) ____   Overall Impression (1-10) ____

SCORE ____

KinnicKinnic

Proof:	86
Age:	NAS
Type:	Not straight
Style:	Blend
Mash Bill:	See comments
Color:	Pale Straw
Price:	$$$$

Mike

Nose: Very odd nose of rotten fruit and Flintstone vitamins.

Taste: Prunes, vanilla, and baking spice. Tastes better that the nose indicates.

Finish: Medium long with oak and spice.

Susan

Nose: Chewable vitamins with a little milk chocolate.

Taste: Vanilla and a sprinkling of sweet spice. Not especially complex.

Finish: After a flash of pepper, quite a bit of the sweetness lingers.

Notes

Great Lakes Distillery, Milwaukee, Wisconsin. Blend of Malt and Rye it produces and a sourced Kentucky straight bourbon. The name is from an Ojibwa word meaning "What is mixed."

My Score

Notes: _____

_____

_____

Appearance (1-5)	____	Nose (1-25)	____
Taste (1-25)	____	Finish (1-25)	____
Complexity (1-10)	____	Overall Impression (1-10)	____

SCORE ____

Little Book

Proof:	118.8
Age:	8 years
Type:	Not straight
Style:	Blend
Mash Bill:	See comments
Color:	Pale Straw
Price:	$$$$$$

Mike

Nose: Caramel, prunes, and oak.

Taste: Very oak forward with caramel, pitted fruits, and baking spices.

Finish: Long with oak and spice.

Susan

Nose: Rye grass, dried fruit, white pepper.

Taste: Spicy rye crackers topped with raisin-prune spread and a dash of pepper.

Finish: The dried fruit lasts and lasts.

Notes

Blended at Jim Beam Distillery, Clermont, Kentucky. Consisting of 8-year Kentucky straight rye, 13-year Canadian rye, and 40-year Canadian whiskey. Each new release is a "chapter." This was Chapter 2 bottled 2018. Developed by Freddie Noe, who was called Little Book by his grandfather, Book Noe.

My Score

Notes: _____

_____

_____

Appearance (1-5) _____   Nose (1-25) _____

Taste (1-25) _____   Finish (1-25) _____

Complexity (1-10) _____   Overall Impression (1-10) _____

SCORE _____

Outryder

Proof:	100
Age:	4 years
Type:	Bottled-in-Bond
Style:	Blend
Mash Bill:	See comments
Color:	Light Amber
Price:	$$$$$

Mike

Nose: Caramel toffee and ripe apple with a little oak.

Taste: Ripe apple, caramel, and baking spices with a hint of leather and oak.

Finish: Long and dry with oak and spice.

Susan

Nose: Candy corn, baked apples, and a whiff of nutmeg.

Taste: Roasted corn with some cocoa, apples, and spice.

Finish: Long and spicy.

Notes

Wyoming Whiskey, Kirby. Wyoming. A blend of stray batches of their wheated bourbon and American whiskey (40% corn, 40% rye, 20% malted barley).

My Score

Notes: _____

_____

_____

Appearance (1-5) _____   Nose (1-25) _____

Taste (1-25) _____   Finish (1-25) _____

Complexity (1-10) _____   Overall Impression (1-10) _____

SCORE _____

Ransom Rye, Barley, Wheat Whiskey

Proof:	93.4
Age:	NAS
Type:	Finished
Style:	Blend
Mash Bill:	See comments
Color:	Very Pale Straw
Price:	$$$$

Mike

Nose: Rye grass, very brandy-like with grapes and berries.

Taste: Rye grass, raisins, vanilla, and oak with a hint of pepper.

Finish: Medium long with oak and a hint of pepper.

Susan

Nose: Rye grass. Aromatics include chocolate, coffee, and caramel with allspice.

Taste: Very spice forward, with nutmeg, allspice, and white pepper followed by sweet vanilla and ripe fruit.

Finish: Very smooth with sweet spices.

Notes

Ransom Wine Co. & Distillery, McMinnville, Oregon. Blend of whiskey sourced from MGP and 7 different whiskeys distilled in Ransom's alembic copper still. Finished in 60 gallon French oak pinot noir barrels.

My Score

Notes: _____

_____

_____

Appearance (1-5) _____   Nose (1-25) _____

Taste (1-25) _____   Finish (1-25) _____

Complexity (1-10) _____   Overall Impression (1-10) _____

SCORE _____

Rieger's Kansas City Whiskey

Proof:	92
Age:	NAS
Type:	Not straight
Style:	Blend
Mash Bill:	Corn, malt, rye, trace of sherry – see notes
Color:	Pale Straw
Price:	$$$$

Mike

Nose: Sherry, vanilla, and corn with a hint of oak.

Taste: Raisins, vanilla, corn husks, a little pepper and oak.

Finish: Long with oak and pepper.

Susan

Nose: Definite sherry note with vanilla, corn, and some rye spice.

Taste: Dark fruit with some cinnamon and caramel.

Finish: Sherry note lingers and is joined by oak.

Notes

J. Rieger & Co., Kansas City, Missouri. This is a blend of at least 7-year-old corn, malt, and rye whiskeys and a little 15-year-old Oloroso sherry from Williams & Humbert Bodega in Jerez, Spain.

My Score

Notes: _____

_____

_____

Appearance (1-5) ____   Nose (1-25) ____

Taste (1-25) ____   Finish (1-25) ____

Complexity (1-10) ____   Overall Impression (1-10) ____

SCORE ____

Tommy Rotter Triple Barrel American Whiskey

Proof: 92
Age: NAS, youngest whiskey used is 1 year old
Type: Finished
Style: Blend
Mash Bill: Not available
Color: Pale Straw
Price: $$$$

Mike
Nose: Caramel with a hint of pears.
Taste: Very thin. Not a lot of flavor. Brown vodka with a hint of wood.
Finish: Short, very short. Slightly woody.

Susan
Nose: Pine cones, vanilla, green apples.
Taste: Very spicy with white pepper, followed by an almost floral sweetness.
Finish: Peppery, drying to oak.

Notes
A blend of two bourbons sourced from Indiana and a sourced Tennessee whiskey. The blend is finished in new French oak barrels. Tommy Rotter Distillery, Buffalo, New York.

My Score
Notes: _____

_____

_____

Appearance (1-5) ____   Nose (1-25) ____
Taste (1-25) ____   Finish (1-25) ____
Complexity (1-10) ____   Overall Impression (1-10) ____
SCORE ____

Additional Blends Releases

Name: _____

Distillery: _____

Proof: _____   **Mash Bill:** _____

Age: _____   _____

Type: _____   **Color:** _____

Style: _____   **Price:** _____

My Score

Notes: _____

_____

_____

Appearance (1-5) ____   Nose (1-25) ____

Taste (1-25) ____   Finish (1-25) ____

Complexity (1-10) ____   Overall Impression (1-10) ____

SCORE ____

Name: _____

Distillery: _____

Proof: _____   **Mash Bill:** _____

Age: _____   _____

Type: _____   **Color:** _____

Style: _____   **Price:** _____

My Score

Notes: _____

_____

_____

Appearance (1-5) ____   Nose (1-25) ____

Taste (1-25) ____   Finish (1-25) ____

Complexity (1-10) ____   Overall Impression (1-10) ____

SCORE ____

CHAPTER FOUR
CORN WHISKEY

Corn whiskey is Kentucky's original whiskey. It was an unaged whiskey made from corn and it is the whiskey that produced the sub-category of Bourbon whiskey by aging the corn whiskey in charred containers. It was a popular whiskey in the years before prohibition. After prohibition, the modern standard of identity created the corn whiskey we know today. It can be aged in either used or uncharred new containers. Most corn whiskey bottled today is unaged, but there are a few that are aged in used barrels. It would be interesting to see a distiller make a corn whiskey aged in used brandy barrels including apple or peach brandy barrels.

Balcones Baby Blue Corn Whiskey

Proof:	92
Age:	NAS
Type:	Not straight
Style:	Corn
Mash Bill:	100% roasted blue corn
Color:	Very, Very Pale Straw
Price:	$$$$

Mike

Nose: Corn and vanilla with a hint of marshmallows and peaches.

Taste: Corn, vanilla, peaches and just a small hint of pepper.

Finish: Short and dry with oak and that hint of pepper.

Susan

Nose: Corn and vanilla with a hint of peaches.

Taste: Vanilla and cashews with frosted cornflakes.

Finish: Sweet with a touch of oak.

Notes

From Balcones Distilling in Waco, Texas.

My Score

Notes: _____

_____

_____

Appearance (1-5) _____   Nose (1-25) _____

Taste (1-25) _____   Finish (1-25) _____

Complexity (1-10) _____   Overall Impression (1-10) _____

SCORE _____

Balcones Brimstone Corn Whiskey

Proof:	106
Age:	NAS
Type:	Smoked
Style:	Corn
Mash Bill:	100% Hopi blue corn
Color:	Straw
Price:	$$$$$

Mike
Nose: Smoke and lots of it.
Taste: Smoke and corn with a little vanilla and oak.
Finish: Long and smoky with a hint of chocolate.

Susan
Nose: Smoke, burnt popcorn, vanilla.
Taste: Very smoky with some vanilla and a bit of apple.
Finish: Smoke and a little cocoa.

Notes
Balcones Distilling, Waco, Texas. Smoked using Texas shrub oak.

My Score

Notes: _____

_____

_____

Appearance (1-5)	____	Nose (1-25)	____
Taste (1-25)	____	Finish (1-25)	____
Complexity (1-10)	____	Overall Impression (1-10)	____

SCORE ____

Balcones True Blue Straight Corn Whiskey

Proof:	100
Age:	NAS
Type:	Straight
Style:	Corn
Mash Bill:	Roasted blue corn
Color:	Dark Straw
Price:	$$$$$

Mike

Nose:	Corn and vanilla. Very simple nose.
Taste:	Corn, vanilla, a little pepper spice, and fruit leading into to some nice oak.
Finish:	Long and dry with oak and a hint of pepper.

Susan

Nose:	Candy corn with some vanilla and a dash of nutmeg.
Taste:	Corn muffin with dark fruit and some peppery spice.
Finish:	Very dry and spicy.

Notes

Balcones Distilling, Waco, Texas.

My Score	
Notes: _____	
_____	
_____	

Appearance (1-5) ____	Nose (1-25) ____
Taste (1-25) ____	Finish (1-25) ____
Complexity (1-10) ____	Overall Impression (1-10) ____
SCORE ____	

George Dickel White Corn Whiskey No. 1

Proof:	91
Age:	NAS
Type:	Not straight
Style:	Corn
Mash Bill:	84% corn, 8% rye, 8% malted barley
Color:	Clear
Price:	$$

Mike
Nose: Corn and a hint of smoke.
Taste: Corn, smoke and pepper.
Finish: Pepper with a touch of smoke.

Susan
Nose: Sweet corn with a hint of fruit.
Taste: Frosted corn flakes with berries.
Finish: Sweet and warm.

Notes
From George Dickel, Tullahoma, Tennessee. Filtered through sugar maple charcoal.

My Score

Notes: _____

_____

_____

Appearance (1-5) _____   Nose (1-25) _____
Taste (1-25) _____   Finish (1-25) _____
Complexity (1-10) _____   Overall Impression (1-10) _____

SCORE _____

Georgia Moon

Proof:	100
Age:	Less than 30 days
Type:	Not straight
Style:	Corn
Mash Bill:	Corn
Color:	Clear
Price:	$

Mike

Nose:	Sweet corn and pears. Very light nose.
Taste:	Corn, a hint of pears, and pepper.
Finish:	Short and peppery.

Susan

Nose:	Sweet corn and pears,
Taste:	Fresh corn sprinkled with sugar. Poached pears.
Finish:	Short and dry.

Notes

The Johnson Distilling Co., Bardstown, Kentucky. Simple, but surprisingly pleasant.

My Score

Notes: _____

_____

_____

Appearance (1-5)	____	Nose (1-25)	____
Taste (1-25)	____	Finish (1-25)	____
Complexity (1-10)	____	Overall Impression (1-10)	____

SCORE ____

Glen Thunder

Proof:	90
Age:	NAS
Type:	Not straight
Style:	Corn
Mash Bill:	80% corn, 20% malted corn
Color:	Clear
Price:	$$

Mike
Nose: Corn and honey.
Taste: Corn, a bit of sweet honey, and pepper.
Finish: Long and peppery.

Susan
Nose: Fresh sweet corn.
Taste: Corn flakes.
Finish: Pleasantly dry with cereal notes.

Notes
From Finger Lakes Distilling in Burnett, New York.

My Score

Notes: _____

_____

_____

Appearance (1-5) ____	Nose (1-25)	____
Taste (1-25) ____	Finish (1-25)	____
Complexity (1-10) ____	Overall Impression (1-10)	____

SCORE ____

Ironroot Hubris

Proof:	120
Age:	24 months
Type:	Straight
Style:	Corn
Mash Bill:	100% corn
Color:	Light Amber
Price:	$$$$

Mike

Nose: Candy corn, caramel, and a hint of pepper.

Taste: Cornmeal and corn with lots of pepper. Water heightens the sweetness.

Finish: Long and peppery with a hint of oak.

Susan

Nose: Sweet corn, apples, oak, and alcohol.

Taste: Corn, corn husk, pepper.

Finish: Lingering, with pepper.

Notes

After sitting, some milk chocolate is released. Limited release. Sometimes released at other proofs, including 117.8. From Ironroot Republic Distillery in Denison, Texas.

My Score		
Notes: _____		
_____		
_____		
Appearance (1-5) ____	Nose (1-25)	____
Taste (1-25) ____	Finish (1-25)	____
Complexity (1-10) ____	Overall Impression (1-10)	____
SCORE ____		

Long Road Corn Whiskey

Proof:	80
Age:	2 years
Type:	Straight
Style:	Corn
Mash Bill:	Corn, rye, winter wheat
Color:	Very Pale Straw
Price:	$$$

Mike

Nose: Cornmeal with a hint of vanilla.

Taste: Corn and vanilla with a hint of pears in the back.

Finish: Long. Sweet corn and a hint of oak, lasting to a nice dry finish.

Susan

Nose: Fresh buttered corn. Some vanilla and sugar.

Taste: Just like the nose with a little sweet spice.

Finish: Pleasant corn and oak. Clean.

Notes

Pleasant light sip, but would like to try this at 100 proof. All grains are Michigan grown. From Long Road Distillers in Grand Rapids, Michigan.

My Score

Notes: _____

_____

_____

Appearance (1-5)	_____	Nose (1-25)	_____
Taste (1-25)	_____	Finish (1-25)	_____
Complexity (1-10)	_____	Overall Impression (1-10)	_____

SCORE _____

MB Roland Corn Whiskey

Proof:	115
Age:	2 years
Type:	Straight
Style:	Corn
Mash Bill:	95% white corn, 5% malted barley
Color:	Light Straw
Price:	$$$$

Mike

Nose: Corn and lots of it with a little honey and floral notes – roses.

Taste: Corn, vanilla, honey, pepper spice and oak.

Finish: Long dry and spicy with oak and pepper.

Susan

Nose: Roasted corn and oak with some toasted almonds.

Taste: Corn pudding, slightly charred at the edges. Some cinnamon and apple.

Finish: Warm and smooth.

Notes

Aged in used bourbon barrels. Released at cask strength so proof may vary. From MB Roland Distillery in Pembroke, Kentucky.

My Score

Notes: _____

_____

_____

Appearance (1-5) ____	Nose (1-25) ____
Taste (1-25) ____	Finish (1-25) ____
Complexity (1-10) ____	Overall Impression (1-10) ____

SCORE ____

Mellow Corn

Proof:	100
Age:	4 years
Type:	Straight
Style:	Corn, Bottled-in-Bond
Mash Bill:	90% corn, 10% rye and malted barley
Color:	Very Pale Straw
Price:	$

Mike

Nose:	Buttered popcorn, vanilla and a hint of pepper.
Taste:	Buttered corn, vanilla, white pepper with a hint of honey.
Finish:	Long. Starts sweet with honey, but gets peppery.

Susan

Nose:	Sweet corn, orange sherbet, sprinklings of spice.
Taste:	Well…mellow; sweet corn, light fruit, white pepper.
Finish:	Corn alcohol and a hint of oak.

Notes

From Heaven Hill, Louisville, Kentucky. Aged in used Heaven Hill bourbon barrels. Notably, it is bottled-in-bond.

My Score

Notes: _____

_____

_____

Appearance (1-5)	____	Nose (1-25)	____
Taste (1-25)	____	Finish (1-25)	____
Complexity (1-10)	____	Overall Impression (1-10)	____
	SCORE ____		

Old 55 Corn Whiskey

Proof:	80
Age:	Unaged
Type:	Not Straight
Style:	Corn
Mash Bill:	Sweet Corn
Color:	Clear
Price:	$$$

Mike

Nose: Corn – Frito corn chip. A hint of pepper.
Taste: Sweet corn and pepper.
Finish: Long and peppery.

Susan

Nose: Ripe corn and sweet alcohol.
Taste: Buttered corn on the cob.
Finish: Dry and spicy.

Notes

From Old 55 Distillery, Newtown, Indiana named after the state highway on which it is located. Distilled from sweet corn grown on the family farm. This was Batch No. 1504, Bottle 23.

My Score

Notes: _____

_____

_____

Appearance (1-5) _____   Nose (1-25) _____

Taste (1-25) _____   Finish (1-25) _____

Complexity (1-10) _____   Overall Impression (1-10) _____

SCORE _____

Additional Corn Whiskey Releases

Name: _____

Distillery: _____

Proof: _____ **Mash Bill:** _____

Age: _____ _____

Type: _____ **Color:** _____

Style: _____ **Price:** _____

My Score		
Notes: _____		
_____		
_____		
Appearance (1-5) ____	Nose (1-25) ____	
Taste (1-25) ____	Finish (1-25) ____	
Complexity (1-10) ____	Overall Impression (1-10) ____	
SCORE ____		

Name: _____

Distillery: _____

Proof: _____ **Mash Bill:** _____

Age: _____ _____

Type: _____ **Color:** _____

Style: _____ **Price:** _____

My Score		
Notes: _____		
_____		
_____		
Appearance (1-5) ____	Nose (1-25) ____	
Taste (1-25) ____	Finish (1-25) ____	
Complexity (1-10) ____	Overall Impression (1-10) ____	
SCORE ____		

Chapter Five
Malt Whiskey

There is a tradition of American Malt Whiskey dating back to the 19th century. Unfortunately, the 19th century malt whiskeys did not have a good reputation. The most famous of the malt whiskeys was "Duffy's Pure Malt Whiskey", which had a reputation of being adulterated with coloring and flavoring just to make it drinkable. Malt whiskey has made a comeback in the 21st century with the artisan distillery movement, and several distilleries are making very good malt whiskeys.

Alpine Traveler's Rest Single Malt

Proof: 90
Age: NAS
Type: Not straight
Style: Malt
Mash Bill: 100% barley
Color: Very Pale Straw
Price: $$$$

Mike

Nose: Lots of malted grain and a little vanilla.
Taste: Vanilla with a hint of berries.
Finish: Dry with some pepper and very light oak.

Susan

Nose: Faint banana and citrus with a bit of malt.
Taste: Banana bread with nuts. Simple, but very pleasant.
Finish: Dries to sweet oak and spice.

Notes

From Alpine Distilling in Park City, Utah. Distilled in copper pot still. Aged in used bourbon barrels and finished in new toasted French oak barrels. May see a 90 proof bottling. There is also a barrel proof expression.

My Score		
Notes: _____		
_____		
_____		
Appearance (1-5) ____	Nose (1-25) ____	
Taste (1-25) ____	Finish (1-25) ____	
Complexity (1-10) ____	Overall Impression (1-10) ____	
SCORE ____		

Balcones Texas Single Malt

Proof: 106
Age: NAS
Type: Not straight
Style: Malt
Mash Bill: 100% barley
Color: Dark straw
Price: $$$$

Mike
Nose: Cherries and dates with brown sugar and malt.
Taste: Cherries with vanilla and malt.
Finish: Long and earthy, almost peaty.

Susan
Nose: Dry maltiness with a little caramel, baked apples, and cherries.
Taste: Sweet malt and caramel with some cherries and smoke.
Finish: Long and dry.

Notes
From Balcones Distilling, Waco, Texas. Very nicely balanced.

My Score		
Notes: _____		
_____		
_____		
Appearance (1-5) _____	Nose (1-25) _____	
Taste (1-25) _____	Finish (1-25) _____	
Complexity (1-10) _____	Overall Impression (1-10) _____	
SCORE _____		

Colkegan American Single Malt Whiskey

Proof:	92
Age:	NAS
Type:	Not straight
Style:	Malt
Mash Bill:	100% malted barley
Color:	Very Pale Straw
Price:	$$$$

Mike

Nose: Very, very light hints of malt and vanilla.
Taste: Lightly peated with vanilla wafers and peat.
Finish: Long and peaty.

Susan

Nose: Faint smoke with some cinnamon and pear.
Taste: Light wood smoke with vanilla and pepper.
Finish: Lingering smoke.

Notes

From Santa Fe Spirits, Santa Fe, New Mexico. The malt is smoked. (Not saying with what, but we suspect some mesquite may be involved.) Also finished in a variety of barrels. A very flavorful sip.

My Score

Notes: _____

_____

_____

Appearance (1-5)	____	Nose (1-25)	____
Taste (1-25)	____	Finish (1-25)	____
Complexity (1-10)	____	Overall Impression (1-10)	____

SCORE ____

Copper Fox Single Malt

Proof:	96
Age:	NAS
Type:	Pot Distilled, Finished
Style:	Malt
Mash Bill:	2-row and 6-row malted barley smoked with applewood and cherrywood
Color:	Dark Straw
Price:	$$$$

Mike

Nose: Malted bread dough, with some smoke and a hint of fruit.

Taste: Smoky with a little iodine, oak and berries.

Finish: Long and smoky.

Susan

Nose: Lots of sweet oak, some vanilla, and a suggestion of fruit.

Taste: Malty with some smoke and vanilla. Perhaps a taste of apple.

Finish: Spicy and dry.

Notes

Copper Fox Distilling Enterprises, Williamsburg and Sperryville, Virginia.

My Score

Notes: _____

_____

_____

Appearance (1-5) _____   Nose (1-25) _____

Taste (1-25) _____   Finish (1-25) _____

Complexity (1-10) _____   Overall Impression (1-10) _____

SCORE _____

Dead Guy Whiskey

Proof:	80
Age:	2 years
Type:	Small Batch
Style:	Malt
Mash Bill:	100 malted barley
Color:	Very Pale Straw
Price:	$$$$

Mike

Nose:	Very malty with some vanilla and grapefruit.
Taste:	Sweet vanilla, oak, and malt. No burn, but pleasant warmth.
Finish:	Short, but dry with a hint of spice.

Susan

Nose:	Light maltiness with some baked apples and some citrus.
Taste:	Very light malt and baked fruit with a touch of oak.
Finish:	Dry with some fruit.

Notes

Rogue Spirits, Portland, Oregon. Distilled with the malted barley used for Rogue Brewing's craft beers. Lightweight, but refreshing.

My Score

Notes: _____

_____

_____

Appearance (1-5)	____	Nose (1-25)	____
Taste (1-25)	____	Finish (1-25)	____
Complexity (1-10)	____	Overall Impression (1-10)	____

SCORE ____

Defiant American Single Malt Whisky

Proof:	82
Age:	NAS
Type:	Not straight
Style:	Malt
Mash Bill:	100% malted two row barley
Color:	Light Straw
Price:	$$$$$

Mike

Nose: Caramel coloring aroma and a little malt.

Taste: Light malt and a little pepper.

Finish: Short and boring.

Susan

Nose: Somehow reminiscent of Coca-Cola with a little bit of maltiness.

Taste: Very faintly malty with caramel.

Finish: Very quick.

Notes

Blue Ridge Distilling Co., Golden Valley, North Carolina. Made in a copper pot still. Aged in stainless steel tanks with oak spirals. This is rather odd, because by the Federal standards of identity this cannot be called "whiskey." The standards clearly state that distillate must "be store in oak containers" to be called whiskey.

My Score

Notes: _____

_____

_____

Appearance (1-5) ____   Nose (1-25) ____

Taste (1-25) ____   Finish (1-25) ____

Complexity (1-10) ____   Overall Impression (1-10) ____

SCORE ____

F.E.W. Single Malt

Proof:	93
Age:	1 year
Type:	Not straight
Style:	Malt
Mash Bill:	100 % malted barley
Color:	Very Pale Straw
Price:	$$$$$

Mike

Nose: Malt, vanilla, and a hint of coffee.

Taste: Malt, vanilla, chocolate, cherries, a hint of spice.

Finish: Medium long with oak and chocolate.

Susan

Nose: Malt and cherries with some tobacco and smoke.

Taste: Enough smokiness it could almost be mistaken for a peated malt. With light cherry fruit, mocha, and oak.

Finish: Very dry and oaky.

Notes

F.E.W. Spirits, Evanston, IL. Aged in rye and bourbon barrels. A little research revealed that the whiskey contains both smoked and non-smoked barley. Ah ha!

My Score

Notes: _____

_____

_____

Appearance (1-5) _____   Nose (1-25) _____

Taste (1-25) _____   Finish (1-25) _____

Complexity (1-10) _____   Overall Impression (1-10) _____

SCORE _____

Garryana Native Oak

Proof:	112
Age:	At least 51 months
Type:	Finished
Style:	Malt
Mash Bill:	5-malt, Washington select, heavily peated malts
Color:	Straw
Price:	$$$$$$

Mike
Nose: Cherries and vanilla with a hint of oak.
Taste: Bubblegum with a little peat and oak.
Finish: Long and peaty.

Susan
Nose: Lightly peaty with caramel, cinnamon, and cherries. Enticing.
Taste: Peat carries through and dominates, but supported by caramel, nutmeg and cherries.
Finish: Long and smoky.

Notes
Third limited release (1600 bottles) from Westland Distillery, Seattle. Finished in a variety of barrels, including Gerry oak (*Quercus garryana*) native to the Pacific Northwest, as well as ex-bourbon, and ex-port.

My Score

Notes: _____

_____

_____

Appearance (1-5)	____	Nose (1-25)	____
Taste (1-25)	____	Finish (1-25)	____
Complexity (1-10)	____	Overall Impression (1-10)	____

SCORE ____

Glen Fargo American Malt Double Barrel

Proof: 94.2
Age: 2 years
Type: Finished
Style: Malt
Mash Bill: Unspecified malted barley
Color: Dark Straw
Price: $$$$$

Mike

Nose: Bourbon caramel with a hint of honey and pitted fruit – cherries or dates.

Taste: Sweet honey and spice. A little white pepper with some dates and oak.

Finish: Short, but peppery with a hint of oak.

Susan

Nose: Barley malt with some unripe peaches and a hint of cocoa.

Taste: Dry and smooth with a bit of vanilla and a hint of cherry sweetness.

Finish: Dry, but not tannic with some lingering fruit.

Notes

From Proof Artisan Distillers of Fargo, North Dakota, Joel Kath is the distiller. Uses locally-farmed barley. Finished in ex-bourbon barrels.

My Score

Notes: _____

_____

_____

Appearance (1-5) ____   Nose (1-25) ____
Taste (1-25) ____   Finish (1-25) ____
Complexity (1-10) ____   Overall Impression (1-10) ____
SCORE ____

Going to the Sun

Proof:	86
Age:	3 years
Type:	Not straight
Style:	Malt
Mash Bill:	100% barley
Color:	Extremely Pale Straw
Price:	$$$ (pint)

Mike

Nose:	French vanilla and hazelnuts with a hint of fruit.
Taste:	Vanilla and peaches with a hint of the hazelnuts and baking spices.
Finish:	Medium long with spice ad nuts.

Susan

Nose:	Banana bread and candied nuts with some light caramel.
Taste:	Much drier than the nose, Vanilla and nuts.
Finish:	Peppery and dry. Nuts linger.

Notes

From Glacier Distilling Company, Coram, Montana. This light sip was a limited release named after the famous road in nearby Glacier National Park. Glacier has a regularly released single malt, the 90 proof Wheatfish. Only available in Montana.

My Score

Notes: _____

_____

_____

Appearance (1-5)	____	Nose (1-25)	____
Taste (1-25)	____	Finish (1-25)	____
Complexity (1-10)	____	Overall Impression (1-10)	____

SCORE ____

Highland Laddie Celtic Whiskey

Proof:	86
Age:	3 years
Type:	Single Barrel, Non-Chill Filtered
Style:	Malt
Mash Bill:	100% barley
Color:	Pale Straw
Price:	$$$$

Mike

Nose:	Caramel and butterscotch with a hint of witch hazel.
Taste:	Cheap dishwashing soap.
Finish:	Very soapy.

Susan

Nose:	Astringent with some oak.
Taste:	Scented dishwashing soap.
Finish:	Soapy!

Notes

From Stonehouse Distillery, Winston, Montana.

My Score

Notes: _____

_____

_____

Appearance (1-5) _____   Nose (1-25) _____

Taste (1-25) _____   Finish (1-25) _____

Complexity (1-10) _____   Overall Impression (1-10) _____

SCORE _____

Kings County American Single Malt

Proof:	94
Age:	2 years
Type:	Peated
Style:	Malt
Mash Bill:	100% barley
Color:	Pale Straw
Price:	$$$$ (375 mL)

KINGS COUNTY DISTILLERY
american whiskey made from peated malt
"single malt"
375ml 47% alcohol by volume

Mike

Nose: Peat and peached with a hint of vanilla and oak.

Taste: Peat with a little peach fruit, vanilla, and cinnamon spice.

Finish: Medium long with oak and spice.

Susan

Nose: Peat and grain with a faint whiff of fruit.

Taste: Peat forward with vanilla pitted fruit, and brown sugar.

Finish: Long and smoky with a little pepper.

Notes

A good, light-bodied "beginner's" peated malt. From Kings County Distillery, Brooklyn, New York.

My Score

Notes: _____

_____

_____

Appearance (1-5) ____   Nose (1-25) ____

Taste (1-25) ____   Finish (1-25) ____

Complexity (1-10) ____   Overall Impression (1-10) ____

SCORE ____

MB Roland Malt

Proof:	108
Age:	2 years
Type:	Straight
Style:	Malt
Mash Bill:	63% malted barley, 21% white corn, 15% rye
Color:	Straw
Price:	$$$$

Mike

Nose: Malt and apples with some vanilla and hazelnuts.

Taste: Vanilla, hazelnuts, and a hint of apples. Lots of pepper spice on the end.

Finish: Long and peppery.

Susan

Nose: Rye co-exists with nutty malt on the nose.

Taste: Vanilla and corn with a lot of malty sweetness along with rye spice and milk chocolate.

Finish: Chocolate really lingers during the finish.

Notes

Mike made a note: "American malt I really like!" Susan found it very impressive for a two-year-old whiskey. Barrel in which it is aged has a Number 4 char.

My Score

Notes: _____

_____

_____

Appearance (1-5)	____	Nose (1-25)	____
Taste (1-25)	____	Finish (1-25)	____
Complexity (1-10)	____	Overall Impression (1-10)	____

SCORE ____

McCarthy's Oregon Single Malt

Proof:	85
Age:	3 years
Type:	Peated
Style:	Malt
Mash Bill:	100% malted Scottish barley
Color:	Very, Very, Very Pale Straw
Price:	$$$$

Mike

Nose: Peat and lots of it. Just a hint of oak and vanilla.

Taste: Peat, a little vanilla and salted caramel.

Finish: Long and peaty.

Susan

Nose: Peat! Some underlying fruitiness peeks through the smoke.

Taste: Peat and interestingly some pasta-like grain, as well as vanilla.

Finish: Fruit becomes more apparent on the finish.

Notes

If you like peat, you'll love this. Distilled in a Holstein pot still at Clear Creek Distillery, Hood River Distillers, Portland. Aged in 100% Oregon oak.

My Score

Notes: _____

_____

_____

Appearance (1-5) _____   Nose (1-25) _____

Taste (1-25) _____   Finish (1-25) _____

Complexity (1-10) _____   Overall Impression (1-10) _____

SCORE _____

McKenzie Pure Pot Still

Proof:	80
Age:	NAS
Type:	Not straight
Style:	Malt
Mash Bill:	Malted barley, unmalted barley, oats
Color:	Very, Very Pale Straw
Price:	$$$$

Mike

Nose: Malt and fruit – berries and pears – with some vanilla.

Taste: Malt vanilla and ripe pears with a little pepper spice and just a hint of oak.

Finish: Short. Starts peppery, but then the malt kicks in.

Susan

Nose: Sweet grain and not much else. Very simple.

Taste: Lots of grain with a little bit of vanilla and citrus.

Finish: Some peppery spice on the finish, which lingers surprisingly. Dries to very light oak.

Notes

From Finger Lakes Distilling, Burdett, New York. Grains are locally sourced.

My Score		
Notes: _____		
_____		
_____		
Appearance (1-5) ____	Nose (1-25) ____	
Taste (1-25) ____	Finish (1-25) ____	
Complexity (1-10) ____	Overall Impression (1-10) ____	
SCORE ____		

O'Danagher's American Hibernian Whiskey

Proof:	90
Age:	5 years
Type:	Single Barrel
Style:	Malt
Mash Bill:	Barley, wheat, oats
Color:	Light Straw
Price:	$$$$$

Mike

Nose: Malt and fruit – apricots – a little vanilla oak.

Taste: Very thin and watery – malt, vanilla, and apricots.

Finish: Long. The oak finally comes out in the finish.

Susan

Nose: Some roasted grain with a whiff of honey and a little malt.

Taste: Multigrain bread with a tiny bit of chocolate and some dried fruit.

Finish: Dry, light, and short.

Notes

Dry Fly Distilling, Spokane, Washington. Whiskey is triple pot distilled. Limited release.

My Score

Notes: _____

_____

_____

Appearance (1-5) _____   Nose (1-25) _____

Taste (1-25) _____   Finish (1-25) _____

Complexity (1-10) _____   Overall Impression (1-10) _____

SCORE _____

Parker's Heritage Malt

Proof:	108
Age:	8 years
Type:	Straight
Style:	Malt
Mash Bill:	65% malted barley, 35% corn
Color:	Straw
Price:	$$$$$$

Mike

Nose: Malt corn with a little vanilla fruit. Water opens the nose and some caramel comes out.

Taste: Caramel, malted milk balls, and apple fruit and oak. Water enhances the caramel making it buttery.

Finish: Dry with oak, vanilla, and baking spices. Water adds some buttery notes to the finish.

Susan

Nose: Alcohol with some beer-like barley notes. Hint of vanilla.

Taste: Dry, with oak, pepper, some vanilla and less malt that one might expect.

Finish: Long and tannic.

Notes

Water tames the alcohol on the nose and releases some apple fruit. Also sweetens the overall taste, but this is still a very dry whiskey.

My Score

Notes: _____

_____

_____

Appearance (1-5)	____	Nose (1-25)	____
Taste (1-25)	____	Finish (1-25)	____
Complexity (1-10)	____	Overall Impression (1-10)	____

SCORE ____

Pearse Lyon's Reserve

Proof:	80
Age:	NAS
Type:	Pot Still
Style:	Malt
Mash Bill:	100% malted barley
Color:	Very, Very Pale Straw
Price:	$$$

Mike

Nose: Malt and vanilla and a hint of fruit.

Taste: Very malty with vanilla and hints of fruit and oak.

Finish: Medium long with that hint of oak.

Susan

Nose: Very fruity. Pears, peaches, apples. A fruit salad.

Taste: Light malt with a note of honey.

Finish: Light, dry, and clean.

Notes

Alltech's Lexington Distilling Company, Lexington, Kentucky. Irish-style malt whiskey made in copper pot stills.

My Score

Notes: _____

_____

_____

Appearance (1-5) _____   Nose (1-25) _____

Taste (1-25) _____   Finish (1-25) _____

Complexity (1-10) _____   Overall Impression (1-10) _____

SCORE _____

Stranahan's Colorado Whiskey

Proof:	94
Age:	2 years minimum
Type:	Straight
Style:	Malt
Mash Bill:	100% malted barley
Color:	Pale Straw
Price:	$$$$$

Mike

Nose: Bread dough and vanilla with a hint of fruit.

Taste: Very light. Vanilla and hazelnuts with a hint of apricot.

Finish: Short and dry with some oak and baking spices – nutmeg and ginger.

Susan

Nose: Classic barley with little vanilla and some pear fruit.

Taste: Very light with some vanilla, but mostly black pepper.

Finish: Warm, drying to oak tannins and spice.

Notes

Stranahan's of Denver, Colorado specialized in single malts. Addition of a little water didn't seem to make any change in the flavor.

My Score

Notes: _____

_____

_____

Appearance (1-5) _____   Nose (1-25) _____

Taste (1-25) _____   Finish (1-25) _____

Complexity (1-10) _____   Overall Impression (1-10) _____

SCORE _____

Stranahan's Diamond Peak

Proof:	94
Age:	4 years minimum
Type:	Straight
Style:	Malt
Mash Bill:	Four different barleys
Color:	Straw
Price:	$$$$$

Mike

Nose: A little fruit – dates and prunes – with some caramel and oak.

Taste: Dates and prunes come through on the palate with caramel and a little medicinal tang.

Finish: Long and medicinal.

Susan

Nose: Sweet malted grain with some apricot/peach aroma.

Taste: Very sweet for a malt whiskey. Fruit salad and sweet malt notes.

Finish: Lingers with sweet oak and some cherries.

Notes

Rob Dietrich, Stranahan's master distiller, selects the barrels to go into this expression. This was batch number 25.

My Score

Notes: _____

_____

_____

Appearance (1-5) ـــــ   Nose (1-25) ـــــ

Taste (1-25) ـــــ   Finish (1-25) ـــــ

Complexity (1-10) ـــــ   Overall Impression (1-10) ـــــ

SCORE ـــــ

Stranahan's Sherry Cask Single Malt

Proof:	94
Age:	4 years minimum
Type:	Finished
Style:	Malt
Mashb Bll:	Four different barleys
Color:	Straw
Price:	$$$$$

Mike

Nose:	Sherry, malt, and a hint of oak.
Taste:	Sherry, malt, vanilla, and baking spice.
Finish:	Very fruity at first, but dries out with some spice.

Susan

Nose:	Ripe peaches, sweet malt, some light spice.
Taste:	Vanilla and cinnamon-dusted apples with malt supplemented with the wine notes.
Finish:	The sherry notes are most present in the finish, accompanied with light tannins.

Notes

The four-year-old whiskey used for Diamond Peak is finished in Oloroso sherry casks.

My Score

Notes: _____

_____

_____

Appearance (1-5)	____	Nose (1-25)	____
Taste (1-25)	____	Finish (1-25)	____
Complexity (1-10)	____	Overall Impression (1-10)	____

SCORE ____

Tom's Foolery Malt

Proof:	100.78
Age:	4 years
Type:	Small Batch
Style:	Malt
Mash Bill:	100% malted barley
Color:	Very Pale Straw
Price:	$$$$

Mike

Nose: Malt and lots of it, with a little vanilla.

Taste: Thin – vanilla, with a little fruit note and a hint of smoke and oak.

Finish: Short, with smoke and oak.

Susan

Nose: Very oaky malt with pecans and an edge of spice.

Taste: Rich malt cereal. Grape Nuts. Velvety mouthfeel.

Finish: Sweet oak lingers.

Notes

Tom's Foolery Distillery, Burton, Ohio. We were sent a barrel proof sample by Tom and Lianne Herbruck, the owners/distillers. The whiskey will be bottled and sold at 90 proof. Photo of a different whiskey, but bottle shape, wax, and logo will be the same.

My Score

Notes: _____

_____

_____

Appearance (1-5)	____	Nose (1-25)	____
Taste (1-25)	____	Finish (1-25)	____
Complexity (1-10)	____	Overall Impression (1-10)	____

SCORE ____

Triple Smoke Single Malt

Proof:	80
Age:	NAS
Type:	Small Batch
Style:	Malt
Mash Bill:	Barley smoked with two woods and peat
Color:	Straw
Price:	$$$$

Mike

Nose: Smoke, of course, with a hint of fruit and vanilla.

Taste: Smoke and vanilla with a little ripe pear fruit and baking spices.

Finish: Very soft smokiness with a hint of oak.

Susan

Nose: Smoky malt with notes of cherry and oak.

Taste: Not as much smoke on the palate as in the nose. Pears, cherries and some nuts predominate.

Finish: Dry and oaky with a whiff of smoke at the end.

Notes

Pot distilled from cherry wood, beechwood, and peat smoked barley. Corsair Distillery, Bowling Green, Kentucky. Batch 97, bottle 361 of 1116.

My Score

Notes: _____

_____

_____

Appearance (1-5) _____   Nose (1-25) _____

Taste (1-25) _____   Finish (1-25) _____

Complexity (1-10) _____   Overall Impression (1-10) _____

SCORE _____

Two Med

Proof:	86
Age:	2 years
Type:	Hopped
Style:	Malt
Mash Bill:	Malted barley and hops
Color:	Straw
Price:	$$$ (375 mL)

Mike

Nose: Maple syrup and pecan pancakes with a hint of oranges.

Taste: Oranges caramel, and baking spices.

Finish: Short with dry oak.

Susan

Nose: Vanilla, aromatic hops flavor, and some light spice and citrus.

Taste: Interesting Scotch-like dryness with lots of spice. Rich mouthfeel.

Finish: Long and spicy with a touch of mint.

Notes

Distilled by Glacier Distilling Company, Coram, Montana from a beer, Good Medicine Strong Red Ale from Great Northern Brewing Company. A very interesting distilling experiment and a tasty sip.

My Score

Notes: _____

_____

_____

Appearance (1-5)	____	Nose (1-25)	____
Taste (1-25)	____	Finish (1-25)	____
Complexity (1-10)	____	Overall Impression (1-10)	____

SCORE ____

Virginia Highland Whisky Chardonnay Cask Finished

Proof:	92
Age:	NAS
Type:	Finished
Style:	Malt
Mash Bill:	100% malted barley
Color:	Nearly clear
Price:	$$$$$

Mike

Nose: Lots of malted grain and a little vanilla.

Taste: Vanilla with a hint of berries.

Finish: Dry with some pepper and very light oak.

Susan

Nose: Sweet malt with a whiff of peat.

Taste: Malt and apples with a little pepper spice.

Finish: Pepper lingers on the tongue.

Notes

From Virginia Distillery Co., Lovingston, Virginia. Virginia whisky is blended with whisky from Scotland and finished the wine barrels.

My Score

Notes: _____

_____

_____

Appearance (1-5) _____   Nose (1-25) _____

Taste (1-25) _____   Finish (1-25) _____

Complexity (1-10) _____   Overall Impression (1-10) _____

SCORE _____

Virginia Highland Whisky Cider Cask Finished

Proof:	92
Age:	NAS
Type:	Finished
Style:	Malt
Mash Bill:	100% malted barley
Color:	Very, Very Pale Straw
Price:	$$$$$

Mike

Nose: Very young. Slight peat and vanilla and not much else.

Taste: Peat and vanilla with some pepper spice.

Finish: Very astringent with peat and oak.

Susan

Nose: Malt and a little vanilla.

Taste: Sweet malt like Grape Nuts cereal. Touch of smoke.

Finish: Dry and warm and a little peppery on the tongue.

Notes

From Virginia Distillery Co., Lovingston, Virginia. Virginia whisky is blended with whisky from Scotland and finished cider barrels sourced from Virginia cider makers. Other expressions are finished in port casks and beer casks.

My Score

Notes: _____

_____

_____

Appearance (1-5) _____   Nose (1-25) _____

Taste (1-25) _____   Finish (1-25) _____

Complexity (1-10) _____   Overall Impression (1-10) _____

SCORE _____

Virginia Highland Whisky Port Cask Finished

Proof: 92
Age: At least 1 year
Type: Special Finish
Style: Malt
Mash Bill: 100% malted barley
Color: Light Copper
Price: $$$ (375 mL)

Mike
Nose: Milk chocolate and berries with a hint of malt and oak.
Taste: Young, but tasty Fruity with some notes of mocha.
Finish: Long and fruity with a hit of oak.

Susan
Nose: A little port with some fruit jam, cherries, and caramel.
Taste: Caramel, light fruit, some smoke and herbs.
Finish: Warm and spicy with dark fruit.

Notes
Distilled by Virginia Distilling, Lovingston, Virginia. This was a bottle from Batch No. 9. Complex for such a young whiskey.

My Score

Notes: _____

_____

_____

Appearance (1-5) _____   Nose (1-25) _____
Taste (1-25) _____   Finish (1-25) _____
Complexity (1-10) _____   Overall Impression (1-10) _____
SCORE _____

Westland Peated American Single Malt

Proof:	92
Age:	At least 2 years
Type:	Peated
Style:	Malt
Mash Bill:	100% malted barley
Color:	Pale Straw
Price:	$$$$$

Mike

Nose: Peat and marshmallows with a hint of oak.

Taste: Peat and apricots with a little vanilla.

Finish: Very peaty with a hint of oak.

Susan

Nose: Lightly smoky, as befits a peated whiskey, and a little vanilla.

Taste: Coal smoke with some brown sugar and apples.

Finish: Smooth, drying to oak and tannins.

Notes

Distilled by Westland Distilling, Seattle, Washington. Lighter than many peated Scotches. Susan is a peat fan and was very pleased. Mike liked it too and thought he would like it even more at 4 years. Non-Chill filtered.

My Score

Notes: _____

_____

_____

Appearance (1-5)	____	Nose (1-25)	____
Taste (1-25)	____	Finish (1-25)	____
Complexity (1-10)	____	Overall Impression (1-10)	____

SCORE ____

Woodford Reserve Five Malt

Proof: 90.4
Age: 6 months
Type: Not straight
Style: Malt
Mash Bill: 5 different beer malts
Color: Barely tinted, almost clear
Price: $$$$ (375 mL)

Mike
Nose: Malt cereal and little else. Very light.
Taste: Very young new make flavor. A little vanilla and cereal grain.
Finish: Short. Very little flavor.

Susan
Nose: Malty with dry cereal notes.
Taste: Surprisingly sweet cereal sprinkled with faint spice.
Finish: Dry and tannic, though a touch of brown sugar and fruit pops up at the very end.

Notes
Woodford Reserve, Versailles, Kentucky. Aged in ex-Woodford reserve Double Oaked barrels. Part of the Distillery Series only sold in the distillery shop. Malts used were two row, wheat, pale chocolate, kiln coffee, carafa.

My Score

Notes: _____

_____

_____

Appearance (1-5) ____   Nose (1-25) ____
Taste (1-25) ____   Finish (1-25) ____
Complexity (1-10) ____   Overall Impression (1-10) ____
SCORE ____

Woodford Reserve Straight Malt

Proof:	90.4
Age:	At least 2 years
Type:	Straight
Style:	Malt
Mash Bill:	51% malted barley, 47% corn, 2% rye
Color:	Pale Straw
Price:	$$$$

Mike

Nose: malted cereal, vanilla, just a hint of oak.
Taste: malted cereal, vanilla, a hint of fruit and oak.
Finish: Short and malty.

Susan

Nose: Sweet malt with corn and light caramel.
Taste: Malted bananas. More caramel with vanilla notes, too.
Finish: Sweet at first and drying to spicy oak.

Notes

Woodford Reserve, Versailles, Kentucky. A beginner's malt for bourbon lovers or a near-bourbon for malt enthusiasts? We would be interested to see what some more age would do for this.

My Score

Notes: _____

_____

_____

Appearance (1-5)	____	Nose (1-25)	____
Taste (1-25)	____	Finish (1-25)	____
Complexity (1-10)	____	Overall Impression (1-10)	____

SCORE ____

Additional Malt Whiskey Releases

Name: _____

Distillery: _____

Proof: _____   **Mash Bill:** _____
Age: _____   _____
Type: _____   **Color:** _____
Style: _____   **Price:** _____

My Score

Notes: _____
_____
_____

Appearance (1-5) ____   Nose (1-25) ____
Taste (1-25) ____   Finish (1-25) ____
Complexity (1-10) ____   Overall Impression (1-10) ____
SCORE ____

Name: _____

Distillery: _____

Proof: _____   **Mash Bill:** _____
Age: _____   _____
Type: _____   **Color:** _____
Style: _____   **Price:** _____

My Score

Notes: _____
_____
_____

Appearance (1-5) ____   Nose (1-25) ____
Taste (1-25) ____   Finish (1-25) ____
Complexity (1-10) ____   Overall Impression (1-10) ____
SCORE ____

CHAPTER SIX
OTHER GRAINS WHISKEY

This has never been a large category for American whiskey. There were a few of them produced in the past, but it is in the 21st century that the category has come upon its own. Many artisan distilleries are experimenting with other grains, such as oats and millet, to create unique whiskeys. They hope to capture the taste of consumers with these whiskeys and thus create a name for themselves in the whiskey market.

Kings County Oated

Proof:	90
Age:	1 year
Type:	Not straight
Style:	Oat Whiskey
Mash Bill:	51% oats
Color:	Amber
Price:	$$$$ (375 mL)

Mike

Nose: Very fruity with raisins and plums with a hint of apricots and leather.

Taste: Surprisingly lighter than the nose indicates. Light apricot and peaches with nutmeg and allspice and a hint of oak.

Finish: Medium long with sweet fruit and spice.

Susan

Nose: Vanilla, caramel, berries, and sweet oak.

Taste: Caraway, oak, and nuts.

Finish: Persistently spicy. Becomes very dry.

Notes

Kings County Distillery, Brooklyn, New York. Would be very interesting to try this in a Manhattan.

My Score

Notes: _____

_____

_____

Appearance (1-5)	____	Nose (1-25)	____
Taste (1-25)	____	Finish (1-25)	____
Complexity (1-10)	____	Overall Impression (1-10)	____
	SCORE ____		

Lion's Pride Dark Millet

Proof:	80
Age:	NAS
Type:	Organic
Style:	Malt
Mash Bill:	100% millet
Color:	Slight tint
Price:	$$$$

Mike

Nose:	New mown hay with a hint of apricots.
Taste:	Grainy, with vanilla and apricots and a little pepper.
Finish:	Medium long with some black pepper.

Susan

Nose:	Newly mown grass, some melon and spice.
Taste:	Sweet grains, like breakfast cereal.
Finish:	Warm breakfast cereal.

Notes

Kovel Distillery, Chicago, Illinois.

My Score

Notes: _____

_____

_____

Appearance (1-5) ____	Nose (1-25) ____	
Taste (1-25) ____	Finish (1-25) ____	
Complexity (1-10) ____	Overall Impression (1-10) ____	

SCORE ____

Lion's Pride Dark Oat

Proof: 80
Age: NAS
Type: Single Barrel
Style: Oat
Mash Bill: 100% oats
Color: Very, Very Pale Straw
Price: $$$$

Mike
Nose: Vanilla and a hint of fruit and oatmeal.
Taste: Vanilla and oatmeal with some fruit and pepper.
Finish: Very short with a hint of pepper.

Susan
Nose: Newly mown grass, some melon and spice.
Taste: Sweet and nutty with some pear.
Finish: Medium long and fruity, ending in some spice.

Notes
Kovel Distillery, Chicago, Illinois. Barrel 130.

My Score

Notes: _____
_____
_____

Appearance (1-5) ____   Nose (1-25) ____
Taste (1-25) ____   Finish (1-25) ____
Complexity (1-10) ____   Overall Impression (1-10) ____
SCORE ____

The One and Only Buckwheat

Proof:	85
Age:	NAS
Type:	Not straight
Style:	Buckwheat
Mash Bill:	80% buckwheat, 20% small grains
Color:	Dark Straw
Price:	$$$$

Mike
Nose: Vanilla and a hint of chocolate and oranges.
Taste: Vanilla, oranges, a little baking spice, and oak.
Finish: Long – orange and oak with a hint of spice.

Susan
Nose: Wheat crackers, nuts, and some brown sugar and cinnamon.
Taste: Very dry with pecans, oak, and a bit of pepper spice.
Finish: Nuts fade and some citrus peeks through on the finish.

Notes
Catskill Distilling Company, Bethel, New York. A flavorful, interesting sip, but technically, not a whiskey. By definition, whiskey must be "distilled from grain." and a grain is the edible seed of grasses in the botanical family Poaceae. Buckwheat is in Polygonaceae.

My Score

Notes: _____

_____

_____

Appearance (1-5)	____	Nose (1-25)	____
Taste (1-25)	____	Finish (1-25)	____
Complexity (1-10)	____	Overall Impression (1-10)	____

SCORE ____

Quinoa Whiskey

Proof:	92
Age:	NAS
Type:	Not straight
Style:	Quinoa
Mash Bill:	80% barley, 20% quinoa
Color:	Pale Straw
Price:	$$$$

Mike

Nose:	Vanilla and peaches with a hint of oak.
Taste:	Vanilla and peaches with baking spice, and oak.
Finish:	Long and dry with oak and nutmeg.

Susan

Nose:	Dry nutty quinoa aroma with faint fruit and spice.
Taste:	More strong nuttiness with some pepper and baking spice.
Finish:	Long with lingering spice.

Notes

Corsair, Nashville, Tennessee and Bowling Green, Kentucky. As is the case with buckwheat, quinoa is not a member of the Poaceae. But, since this is made with 80% barley, which is, this spirit qualifies as a whiskey. The nuttiness is very appealing.

My Score

Notes: _____

_____

_____

Appearance (1-5)	____	Nose (1-25)	____
Taste (1-25)	____	Finish (1-25)	____
Complexity (1-10)	____	Overall Impression (1-10)	____

SCORE ____

Straight Triticale Whiskey

Proof:	88
Age:	NAS
Type:	Straight
Style:	Triticale
Mash Bill:	100% triticale
Color:	Very Pale Straw
Price:	$$$$

Mike
Nose: Vanilla and banana pudding with a hint of lemon.

Taste: Vanilla and citrus with some cinnamon spice.

Finish: Dry and spicy with only a hint of oak.

Susan
Nose: Ripe peaches and multigrain cereal.

Taste: Herbal and spicy with a hint of root beer and more peaches.

Finish: Tongue-tingling spicy.

Notes
Dry Fly Distilling, Spokane, Washington. Pot distilled. Triticale is a hybrid grain of rye and wheat.

My Score

Notes: _____

_____

_____

Appearance (1-5) _____   Nose (1-25) _____

Taste (1-25) _____   Finish (1-25) _____

Complexity (1-10) _____   Overall Impression (1-10) _____

SCORE _____

Additional Other Grains Whiskey Releases

Name: _____

Distillery: _____

Proof: _____ **Mash Bill:** _____

Age: _____ _____

Type: _____ **Color:** _____

Style: _____ **Price:** _____

My Score

Notes: _____

_____

_____

Appearance (1-5) _____ Nose (1-25) _____

Taste (1-25) _____ Finish (1-25) _____

Complexity (1-10) _____ Overall Impression (1-10) _____

SCORE _____

Name: _____

Distillery: _____

Proof: _____ **Mash Bill:** _____

Age: _____ _____

Type: _____ **Color:** _____

Style: _____ **Price:** _____

My Score

Notes: _____

_____

_____

Appearance (1-5) _____ Nose (1-25) _____

Taste (1-25) _____ Finish (1-25) _____

Complexity (1-10) _____ Overall Impression (1-10) _____

SCORE _____

Chapter Seven
Rye Whiskey

Rye whiskey is America's first whiskey. It was first distilled in 1648 in Salem, Massachusetts by Emmanuel Downing. It was popular in the northeastern states where rye grew better than corn. Pennsylvania and Maryland became well known producers of rye whiskey in the 19th century. The decline of the production of rye in those states started after prohibition and by the 1990s rye was only being produced in Kentucky and Indiana. This has changed in the 21st century with the rise of the artisan distillery movement.

Rye has grown as a category as artisan distilleries started to make rye whiskey and after the Seagram Distillery in Lawrenceburg, Indiana was sold and the new owners (MGP) made their aging stocks of rye available to the market. Many distillers have used this rye whiskey to create brands, and it is found under many labels today.

77 Whiskey Local Rye & Corn

Proof:	90
Age:	505 days
Type:	Not straight
Style:	Rye
Mash Bill:	85% rye, 15% corn
Color:	Straw
Price:	$$$$

Mike

Nose: Vanilla, ripe apples and bananas, with a hint of oak.

Taste: Vanilla, a hint of liquorice, apples, and oak.

Finish: Long and spicy with liquorice and pepper.

Susan

Nose: Cellulose, rye spice, some dark fruit.

Taste: Lots of light oak, some brown sugar, liquorice, and bananas.

Finish: Long and dry.

Notes

Breuckelen Distilling, Brooklyn, New York. All grown locally sourced from a farmer named Thor. How delightful is that?

My Score

Notes: _____

_____

_____

Appearance (1-5) ____   Nose (1-25) ____

Taste (1-25) ____   Finish (1-25) ____

Complexity (1-10) ____   Overall Impression (1-10) ____

SCORE ____

A.D. Laws Secale Straight Rye Whiskey

Proof:	100
Age:	4 years
Type:	Bottled-in-Bond
Style:	Rye
Mash Bill:	95% rye, 5% malted barley
Color:	Straw
Price:	$$$$$

Mike

Nose: Rye grass and molasses with a hint of oak and spice.

Taste: Rye grass, molasses, some baking spice, and oak.

Finish: Medium long. Starts sweet and then oak kicks in to give it a slightly dry ending.

Susan

Nose: Caraway seed and black pepper.

Taste: Caraway, caramel, and some cherries and berries.

Finish: Spicy with a rich mouthfeel.

Notes

Laws Whiskey House, Denver, Colorado. *Secale* is the genus name for rye. Very well-rounded sip. This was from Batch C17F. All grains used grown in Colorado.

My Score

Notes: _____

_____

_____

Appearance (1-5) _____   Nose (1-25) _____

Taste (1-25) _____   Finish (1-25) _____

Complexity (1-10) _____   Overall Impression (1-10) _____

SCORE _____

Angel's Envy Rye

Proof: 100
Age: NAS
Type: Finished
Style: Rye
Mash Bill: 95% rye, 5% malted barley
Color: Light Amber
Price: $$$$$

Mike

Nose: Cotton candy and molasses dominate the nose, with only a hint of rye whiskey in the aroma.

Taste: Cotton candy and brown sugar with only a hint of rye spice and grain and a little cherry fruit in the background.

Finish: Long and sweet. Rum flavor dominates the finish.

Susan

Nose: New leather, apples, and vanilla. Surprisingly sweet for a rye.

Taste: Burnt marshmallows and molasses.

Finish: Warm and full. Definite sweet rum note on the end.

Notes

Louisville Spirits Group, Louisville, Kentucky. Aged in ex-rum casks and you can certainly taste it! Very sweet for a rye. Dessert rye?

My Score

Notes: _____

_____

_____

Appearance (1-5) ____   Nose (1-25) ____

Taste (1-25) ____   Finish (1-25) ____

Complexity (1-10) ____   Overall Impression (1-10) ____

SCORE ____

Bad Rock Rye

Proof:	118
Age:	3 years
Type:	Barrel Strength, Single Barrel
Style:	Rye
Mash Bill:	Rye, rye malt, corn
Color:	Amber
Price:	$$$$$

Mike

Nose: Very fruity – peaches, apricots, cherries – with vanilla and bread dough.

Taste: Very brandy-like with peaches, dates, caramel, and oak.

Finish: Long and dry with oak and only a hint of sweet fruit.

Susan

Nose: Lots of dry cereal with vanilla and berries.

Taste: Vanilla and caramel with some cinnamon and stewed fruit. Vary some at 118 proof.

Finish: Long and smooth with sweet oak.

Notes

Glacier Distilling, Coram, Montana. This bottle was from Batch 18F11. Nicely balanced.

My Score

Notes: _____

_____

_____

Appearance (1-5) _____   Nose (1-25) _____

Taste (1-25) _____   Finish (1-25) _____

Complexity (1-10) _____   Overall Impression (1-10) _____

SCORE _____

Balcones Texas Rye Whiskey

Proof: 100
Age: NAS
Type: Pot Still
Style: Rye
Mash Bill: 100% rye, 80% grown in Texas
Color: Dark Straw
Price: $$$$

Mike

Nose: Caramel, rye grass, and ripe apricots.
Taste: Carmel, rye grass, pepper spice, and apricots.
Finish: Long, dry, and peppery.

Susan

Nose: Lots of herbal rye grass and notable chocolate. Quite spicy.
Taste: Caraway, herbs, pepper and some underlying chocolate.
Finish: Caramel and some chocolate at the beginning before drying to peppery oak.

Notes

Balcones Distilling, Waco, Texas. Very pleasing rye at a good price. There is also a cask strength expression.

My Score

Notes: _____

_____

_____

Appearance (1-5) _____   Nose (1-25) _____

Taste (1-25) _____   Finish (1-25) _____

Complexity (1-10) _____   Overall Impression (1-10) _____

SCORE _____

Bare Knuckle Rye

Proof:	90
Age:	18 months
Type:	Not straight
Style:	Rye
Mash Bill:	100% rye
Color:	Pale Straw
Price:	$$$$

Mike

Nose:	Vanilla with a hint of banana pudding.
Taste:	Rye grass, vanilla, and bananas.
Finish:	Medium long with some oak.

Susan

Nose:	New leather, rye grass, a suggestion of fruit and nuts.
Taste:	Leather like a new saddle with some rye spice and dark fruit.
Finish:	Medium long and peppery.

Notes

KO Distilling, Manassas, Virginia. There's a cask strength expression, too.

My Score

Notes: _____

_____

_____

Appearance (1-5) _____   Nose (1-25) _____

Taste (1-25) _____   Finish (1-25) _____

Complexity (1-10) _____   Overall Impression (1-10) _____

SCORE _____

Bare Knuckle Single Barrel Rye

Proof:	128.2
Age:	32 months
Type:	Barrel Strength
Style:	Rye
Mash Bill:	100% Virginia rye
Color:	Light Amber
Price:	$$$$$

Mike

Nose: Fruity with prunes and raisins with some caramel and a hint of oak.

Taste: Fruit forward – prunes and raisons with a hint of berries – also vanilla and white pepper.

Finish: Medium long with pepper and a touch of oak.

Susan

Nose: Rye crisp and a little caramel with apples and a very dry pepper that tastes like wild carrot seeds.

Taste: Caramel and dark cherries and pepper spice. (Water reveals some cloves and tobacco.)

Finish: Lingering rye crisp and dark fruit.

Notes

KO Distilling, Manassas, Virginia. Barrel 16-023. Very smooth sip at this high proof.

My Score

Notes: _____

_____

_____

Appearance (1-5) _____   Nose (1-25) _____

Taste (1-25) _____   Finish (1-25) _____

Complexity (1-10) _____   Overall Impression (1-10) _____

SCORE _____

Basil Hayden's Dark Rye Whiskey

Proof:	80
Age:	NAS
Type:	Blend
Style:	Rye
Mash Bill:	See comments
Color:	Dark Amber
Price:	$$$$

Mike

Nose: Caramel, berries and a hint of almonds and old leather.

Taste: Caramel, prunes and berries, with some almonds.

Finish: Long. Starts sweet but dries out with some oak.

Susan

Nose: Sweet with fruity port wine note and some caramel and cinnamon.

Taste: Very smooth with herbal rye sweetened by the port fruit. Notes of cardamom and baked apple as well as some honey.

Finish: Light and lingering.

Notes

Jim Beam Distillery, Clermont, Kentucky. Beam's take on a Maryland-style rye. Though it chose to blend their whiskey with Canadian rye form the Alberta Distillery along with a little California port.

My Score

Notes: _____

_____

_____

Appearance (1-5) _____   Nose (1-25) _____

Taste (1-25) _____   Finish (1-25) _____

Complexity (1-10) _____   Overall Impression (1-10) _____

SCORE _____

Basil Hayden's Rye Whiskey

Proof:	80
Age:	NAS
Type:	Finished
Style:	Rye
Mash Bill:	Probably just barely 51% rye
Color:	Pale Straw
Price:	$$$$

Mike
Nose: Cherries and vanilla with rye grass.
Taste: Rye grass, vanilla and honey with a hint of berries and cherries.
Finish: Short and dry with oak and pepper.

Susan
Nose: Rye grass, sweet mint, and a suggestion of cinnamon.
Taste: Rye spice with vanilla and cinnamon.
Finish: Dries to lightly spicy oak.

Notes
Jim Beam Distillery, Clermont, Kentucky. Rebarreled in new charred oak quarter casks. Would make a good "beginner's" rye. Light and clean.

My Score

Notes: _____

_____

_____

Appearance (1-5) _____   Nose (1-25) _____

Taste (1-25) _____   Finish (1-25) _____

Complexity (1-10) _____   Overall Impression (1-10) _____

SCORE _____

Benjamin Prichard's Tennessee Rye

Proof:	86
Age:	"Less than 4 years"
Type:	Not straight
Style:	Rye
Mash Bill:	70% rye, 15% white corn, 15% malted barley
Color:	Very Pale Straw
Price:	$$$$$

Mike

Nose: Very light nose. Rye grass and vanilla.

Taste: Rye grass, vanilla, and a hint of mint.

Finish: Short with almost no finish. Brown vodka.

Susan

Nose: Mint with undertones of rye grass.

Taste: More mint with herbal notes and vanilla appearing mid-palate.

Finish: Quickly dries to a vanishing point.

Notes

Prichard's Distillery, Kelso, Tennessee. Sourced from Indiana.

My Score

Notes: _____

_____

_____

Appearance (1-5) _____   Nose (1-25) _____

Taste (1-25) _____   Finish (1-25) _____

Complexity (1-10) _____   Overall Impression (1-10) _____

SCORE _____

Blackback Rye Whiskey

Proof:	86
Age:	13 months
Type:	Not straight
Style:	Rye
Mash Bill:	Not released
Color:	Straw
Price:	$$$$

Mike

Nose: Rye grass, raisins, with a little oak and spice.

Taste: Rye grass, raisins, and dates with a little sweet baking spice and oak.

Finish: Medium long with some oak and fruit.

Susan

Nose: Fruity, with rye grass and vanilla.

Taste: Vanilla, oak, rye spice, and pralines.

Finish: Nutty and lingering.

Notes

Silverback Distilling, Afton, Virginia. Bottle 124 of Batch 16. Almost brandy-like. Impressive for such a young whiskey.

My Score

Notes: _____

_____

_____

Appearance (1-5) _____   Nose (1-25) _____

Taste (1-25) _____   Finish (1-25) _____

Complexity (1-10) _____   Overall Impression (1-10) _____

SCORE _____

Bower Hill Reserve Rye

Proof:	86
Age:	NAS
Type:	Straight, Small Batch
Style:	Rye
Mash Bill:	Not disclosed
Color:	Pale Straw
Price:	$$$$$

Mike

Nose: Rye grass, vanilla, and ripe apple.

Taste: Rye grass, vanilla, apples, and pepper spice.

Finish: Short, with a bit of oak and pepper.

Susan

Nose: Dark roast rye seeds, very herbal.

Taste: Very vegetative. No fruit, but some herbs, including dill.

Finish: Short and dry.

Notes

Bower Hill Distilling, Silverton, Ohio.

My Score

Notes: _____

_____

_____

Appearance (1-5) _____   Nose (1-25) _____

Taste (1-25) _____   Finish (1-25) _____

Complexity (1-10) _____   Overall Impression (1-10) _____

SCORE _____

Bulleit 12-Year Rye

Proof:	92
Age:	12 years
Type:	Straight, Extra Aged
Style:	Rye
Mash Bill:	Not disclosed
Color:	Dark Straw
Price:	$$$$

Mike

Nose:	Rye grass, caramel and a hint of ripe apple.
Taste:	Rye grass, caramel, apples, with baking spice and oak.
Finish:	Medium long with oak, spice and a hint of mint.

Susan

Nose:	Rye grass, dark cherries, a bit of cola.
Taste:	Herbal rye notes with cherry cola and some caramel. A flash of mint.
Finish:	Peppery and oaky.

Notes

Diageo, NA. Distilled by MGP, Lawrenceburg, Indiana. The most complex of the Bulleit Rye expressions we sampled.

My Score

Notes: _____

_____

_____

Appearance (1-5)	____	Nose (1-25)	____
Taste (1-25)	____	Finish (1-25)	____
Complexity (1-10)	____	Overall Impression (1-10)	____

SCORE ____

Bulleit Rye

Proof:	95
Age:	NAS
Type:	Straight, Small Batch
Style:	Rye
Mash Bill:	95% rye, 5% malted barley
Color:	Pale Straw
Price:	$$$

Mike

Nose: Spearmint and rye grass with a hint of oak.

Taste: Spearmint, rye grass, vanilla, and baking spices with a hint of oak.

Finish: Long and minty.

Susan

Nose: Mint, leather, caramel, and something floral. (Wild rose?)

Taste: Rye grass, leather, mint.

Finish: Medium long with that lingering mint note.

Notes

Diageo. Currently sourced from MGP in Lawrenceburg, Indiana, but will be made at the new Bulleit Distillery in Shelby County, Kentucky. If you don't care for mint in your whiskey, stay away from this one. If you like it, you will love this.

My Score

Notes: _____

_____

_____

Appearance (1-5) _____   Nose (1-25) _____

Taste (1-25) _____   Finish (1-25) _____

Complexity (1-10) _____   Overall Impression (1-10) _____

SCORE _____

Buzzard's Roost
Single Barrel Rye

Proof:	105
Age:	36 months
Type:	Straight
Style:	Rye
Mash Bill:	Not released
Color:	Straw
Price:	$$$$$

Mike

Nose: Rye grass, vanilla with a hint of fruit and spice.

Taste: Rye grass, vanilla, baking spices, pears, and oak.

Finish: Long and dry with oak and spice.

Susan

Nose: Pears (!) and ripe apples with rye spice and a dash of cinnamon.

Taste: Apples and pears with vanilla, rye grass, cinnamon, and a dollop of caramel.

Finish: Long and warm with rye spice and lingering fruit. Not at all hot.

Notes

Buzzard's Roost Sippin' Whiskeys, Sparta, Kentucky. Sourced from MGP, Lawrenceburg, Indiana. The producer will also be releasing a small batch expression finished in barrels with customized staves.

My Score

Notes: _____

_____

_____

Appearance (1-5) ____ Nose (1-25) ____

Taste (1-25) ____ Finish (1-25) ____

Complexity (1-10) ____ Overall Impression (1-10) ____

SCORE ____

Buzzard's Roost Very Small Batch Straight Rye

Proof:	105
Age:	36 months
Type:	Finished
Style:	Rye
Mash Bill:	Not released
Color:	Dark Straw
Price:	$$$$$

Mike

Nose: Vanilla with a hint of milk chocolate, cherries, rye grass, and oak.

Taste: Vanilla, rye grass, pepper spice, oak, and a hint of berries.

Finish: Long, dry, with oak and pepper.

Susan

Nose: Sweet rye grass and herbs at first. Then it blossoms into figgy pudding with hard sauce.

Taste: Very cognac-like, with dark fruit and herbs.

Finish: Long and spicy.

Notes

Buzzard's Roost Sippin' Whiskeys, Sparta, Kentucky. Sourced from MGP, Lawrenceburg, Indiana. Expression finished in oak barrels with customized, grooved staves. Water sweetens it considerably.

My Score

Notes: _____

_____

_____

Appearance (1-5) ____	Nose (1-25)	____
Taste (1-25) ____	Finish (1-25)	____
Complexity (1-10) ____	Overall Impression (1-10)	____
	SCORE ____	

Cask & Crew

Proof:	80
Age:	See comments
Type:	Blend
Style:	Rye
Mash Bill:	51% Canadian rye, 49% Kentucky corn whiskey
Color:	Light Straw
Price:	$$$$$

Mike

Nose: French vanilla and corn. Very little else.

Taste: Vanilla and corn with a slight hint of oak.

Finish: Very short with only a hint of sweetness.

Susan

Nose: Rye grass, some vanilla, very herbal.

Taste: Rye bread with some corn flakes and a shade of vanilla.

Finish: Some dark fruit emerges at the very end of a short finish.

Notes

LiDestri Beverages, Rochester, New York. The rye in this is 3 years old.

My Score

Notes: _____

_____

_____

Appearance (1-5) ____		Nose (1-25)	____
Taste (1-25) ____		Finish (1-25)	____
Complexity (1-10) ____		Overall Impression (1-10)	____

SCORE ____

Catcher's Rye

Proof: 98.8
Age: 2 years
Type: Straight
Style: Rye
Mash Bill: 100% Michigan rye
Color: Pale Straw
Price: $$$$

Mike

Nose: Rye grass, fruit, and honeysuckle flowers.
Taste: Rye grass, honey, apricots, and pepper spice.
Finish: Very long and spicy.

Susan

Nose: Lots of rye grass with a little vanilla and oak.
Taste: Much sweeter than the nose with caraway and vanilla.
Finish: Warm and sweet drying to soft oak tannins.

Notes

Two James Spirits, Detroit, Michigan. Distilled with water from the Great Lakes. First legal distillery in Detroit since Prohibition.

My Score		
Notes: _____		
_____		
_____		
Appearance (1-5) ____	Nose (1-25)	____
Taste (1-25) ____	Finish (1-25)	____
Complexity (1-10) ____	Overall Impression (1-10)	____
SCORE ____		

Catoctin Creek Roundstone Rye

Proof:	80
Age:	NAS
Type:	Not straight
Style:	Rye
Mash Bill:	100% rye
Color:	Straw
Price:	$$$$

Mike

Nose: Very fruity with ripe peaches and apricots, a hint of vanilla, and oak. Very brandy-like.

Taste: Rye grass, vanilla, and peaches with a little nutmeg and cinnamon.

Finish: Medium long and fruity.

Susan

Nose: Rich herbal rye note with caramel and leather. Some fruit.

Taste: Lightly spicy rye, baking spices and sweet oak with a rich mouthfeel for 80 proof whiskey.

Finish: Starts sweet and dries to smooth spices and oak.

Notes

Catoctin Creek Distilling. Purcellville, Virginia. Very nice mouthfeel for 80 proof.

My Score

Notes: _____

_____

_____

Appearance (1-5) _____   Nose (1-25) _____

Taste (1-25) _____   Finish (1-25) _____

Complexity (1-10) _____   Overall Impression (1-10) _____

SCORE _____

Catoctin Creek Roundstone Rye Cask Proof

Proof:	116
Age:	NAS
Type:	Cask Strength, Single Barrel
Style:	Rye
Mash Bill:	100% rye
Color:	Light Amber
Price:	$$$$$

Mike

Nose: Rye grass, apricots and peaches with some oak and spice.

Taste: Rye grass and spices – nutmeg and cinnamon – with hints of white pepper, apricots, and oak.

Finish: Long and dry with oak and spice.

Susan

Nose: Surprisingly light for cask strength. Lots of rye spice though, with some wood smoke and leather.

Taste: Chewy mouthful. More rye and spice. Water releases the caramel, dark fruit, and a little cinnamon.

Finish: Long and spicy.

Notes

Catoctin Creek Distilling. Purcellville, Virginia.

My Score

Notes: _____

_____

_____

Appearance (1-5)	____	Nose (1-25)	____
Taste (1-25)	____	Finish (1-25)	____
Complexity (1-10)	____	Overall Impression (1-10)	____

SCORE ____

Catoctin Creek Roundstone Rye Distiller's Select

Proof:	92
Age:	NAS
Type:	Single Barrel
Style:	Rye
Mash Bill:	100% rye
Color:	Dark Straw
Price:	$$$$

Mike

Nose: Rye grass, butterscotch, and a hint of fruit.

Taste: Rye grass, caramel, and apricots with some allspice.

Finish: Medium long with oak and spice.

Susan

Nose: Caramel, stone fruit, rye flour.

Taste: Spicy rye with caramel, some mint, and a touch of honey.

Finish: Long and dry with a dash of black pepper at the end.

Notes

Catoctin Creek Distilling, Purcellville, Virginia. Head distiller Becky Harris sets aside 10% of the barrels she makes to use for this rye.

My Score

Notes: _____

_____

_____

Appearance (1-5) ____		Nose (1-25) ____
Taste (1-25) ____		Finish (1-25) ____
Complexity (1-10) ____		Overall Impression (1-10) ____

SCORE ____

Catskill Straight Rye Whiskey

Proof:	85
Age:	NAS
Type:	Straight
Style:	Rye
Mash Bill:	95% rye, 5% malted barley
Color:	Light Amber
Price:	$$$$

Mike

Nose:	Rye grass, vanilla, and pears with a hint of oak.
Taste:	Vanilla and a lot of it. Rye grass and hints of pear and oak.
Finish:	Moderately long with oak and some baking spices.

Susan

Nose:	Caramel, pears, some rye spice.
Taste:	More rye on the palate than the nose. Pepper, orchard fruit, burnt toffee.
Finish:	Dry and peppery.

Notes

Catskill Distilling Company, Bethel, New York.

My Score

Notes: _____

_____

_____

Appearance (1-5) _____   Nose (1-25) _____

Taste (1-25) _____   Finish (1-25) _____

Complexity (1-10) _____   Overall Impression (1-10) _____

SCORE _____

Cody Road Rye

Proof:	80
Age:	NAS
Type:	Not straight
Style:	Rye
Mash Bill:	100% local rye
Color:	Very Pale Straw
Price:	$$$$

Mike

Nose:	Rye grass, floor wax.
Taste:	Rye grass, vanilla, a hint of peaches. Tastes better than it smells.
Finish:	Short and sweet.

Susan

Nose:	Rye grass, cellulose tape, faint spice.
Taste:	Rye bread, a dash of pepper, and some oak.
Finish:	Pepper and oak.

Notes

Mississippi River Distilling Co., Le Claire, Iowa, the hometown of William "Buffalo Bill" Cody. Not complex.

My Score

Notes: _____

_____

_____

Appearance (1-5)	____	Nose (1-25)	____
Taste (1-25)	____	Finish (1-25)	____
Complexity (1-10)	____	Overall Impression (1-10)	____
	SCORE ____		

Col. E.H. Taylor Straight Rye

Proof:	100
Age:	At least 4 years
Type:	Bottled-in-Bond
Style:	Rye
Mash Bill:	Rye and malted barley
Color:	Light Smber
Price:	$$$$

Mike

Nose:	Rye grass, apples, and caramel with baking spices and oak.
Taste:	Rye grass and candy apples with lots of caramel and baking spices, especially cinnamon.
Finish:	Long and dry with oak and cinnamon.

Susan

Nose:	Honey, caramel, spiced pears, and peaches.
Taste:	Rich caramel sauce with cinnamon and pears. Touch of chocolate, too.
Finish:	Long and spicy ending in sweet oak.

Notes

Buffalo Trace Distillery, Frankfort, Kentucky. Yet another wonderful whiskey from Buffalo Trace that we wish they could make in greater quantity. Limited release.

My Score

Notes: _____

_____

_____

Appearance (1-5)	____	Nose (1-25)	____
Taste (1-25)	____	Finish (1-25)	____
Complexity (1-10)	____	Overall Impression (1-10)	____

SCORE ____

Copper Fox Rye

Proof:	90
Age:	NAS
Type:	Pot Distilled, Finished
Style:	Rye
Mash Bill:	2/3 rye, 1/3 malted barley
Color:	Straw
Price:	$$$$

Mike

Nose: Lots of malt and bread dough, a hint of smoke, with apples and a little berry fruit.

Taste: Vanilla and smoke with a hint of iodine, some apple and pepper spice.

Finish: Long with smoke and pepper.

Susan

Nose: Full rye grain with some oak and pepper.

Taste: Rye grass, caraway, tobacco, and oak.

Finish: Long with a persistent tobacco note ending in oak tannins.

Notes

Copper Fox Distilling Enterprises, Williamsburg and Sperryville, Virginia. Aged with applewood and cherry wood chips in ex-bourbon barrels.

My Score

Notes: _____

_____

_____

Appearance (1-5)	____	Nose (1-25)	____
Taste (1-25)	____	Finish (1-25)	____
Complexity (1-10)	____	Overall Impression (1-10)	____

SCORE ____

Dad's Hat 4-Year

Proof:	95
Age:	4 years
Type:	Straight
Style:	Rye
Mash Bill:	80% rye, 20% malted barley
Color:	Very Dark Straw
Price:	$$$$$

Mike

Nose: Rye grass, vanilla, and very ripe peaches with a hint of oak.

Taste: Rye grass, peaches, vanilla cream, and pepper spice.

Finish: Long and spicy with pepper and just a hint of oak.

Susan

Nose: Rye crisp and caraway seeds with some sweet nuts and ripe apples.

Taste: Very rich mouthfeel. Coats the tongue. More rye crackers with peppery spice.

Finish: Long and spicy. The rich mouthfeel lingers for a long time, too.

Notes

Mountain Laurel Spirits, LLC. Grundy Mill Distillery, Bristol, Pennsylvania. Uses "pre-Prohibition style" sweet mash process.

My Score

Notes: _____

_____

_____

Appearance (1-5) _____   Nose (1-25) _____

Taste (1-25) _____   Finish (1-25) _____

Complexity (1-10) _____   Overall Impression (1-10) _____

SCORE _____

Dad's Hat 90 Proof

Proof:	90
Age:	6 months
Type:	Small Batch
Style:	Rye
Mash Bill:	80% rye, 20% malted barley
Color:	Pale Straw
Price:	$$$$

Mike

Nose: Rye grass, vanilla, and a hint of citrus.

Taste: Rye grass, vanilla, citrus, and baking spices with a hint of oak.

Finish: Short, but dry with oak and spice.

Susan

Nose: Lots of herbal rye character with some barn loft and light pepper.

Taste: Pleasantly herbal and spicy with some vanilla and oak.

Finish: Short and spicy.

Notes

Mountain Laurel Spirits, LLC. Grundy Mill Distillery, Bristol, Pennsylvania.

My Score

Notes: _____

_____

_____

Appearance (1-5) _____   Nose (1-25) _____

Taste (1-25) _____   Finish (1-25) _____

Complexity (1-10) _____   Overall Impression (1-10) _____

SCORE _____

Dad's Hat Bonded

Proof:	100
Age:	At least 4 years
Type:	Bottled-in-Bond
Style:	Rye
Mash Bill:	80% rye, 20% malted barley
Color:	Straw
Price:	$$$$

Mike
Nose:	Rye grass and yeast, vanilla and apple blossoms.
Taste:	Rye grass, vanilla, pepper spice, and a hint of apples.
Finish:	Long and spicy.

Susan
Nose:	Rye grass, caraway, and some toffee.
Taste:	Burnt toffee, caramel, dried fruit, black pepper, and oak.
Finish:	The herbal rye notes linger throughout the finish.

Notes
Mountain Laurel Spirits, LLC. Grundy Mill Distillery, Bristol, Pennsylvania.

My Score

Notes: _____

_____

_____

Appearance (1-5) ____   Nose (1-25) ____

Taste (1-25) ____   Finish (1-25) ____

Complexity (1-10) ____   Overall Impression (1-10) ____

SCORE ____

Defiant Rye

Proof:	93
Age:	NAS
Type:	Not straight
Style:	Rye
Mash Bill:	100% rye
Color:	Straw
Price:	$$$$$

Mike

Nose:	Rotting vegetation, which lessens as it opens up in the glass. Then rye grass, vanilla, and honey.
Taste:	Rye grass, vanilla, and a hint of oak.
Finish:	Long and dry.

Susan

Nose:	Rye grass, cellulose, and pepper spice.
Taste:	Rye grass, oak, pepper. Quite hot for the proof.
Finish:	Oak and pepper with a bit of vanilla at the very end.

Notes

Blue Ridge Distilling Company, Golden Valley, North Carolina.

My Score

Notes: _____

_____

_____

Appearance (1-5)	____	Nose (1-25)	____
Taste (1-25)	____	Finish (1-25)	____
Complexity (1-10)	____	Overall Impression (1-10)	____

SCORE ____

District Made Straight Rye Whiskey

Proof:	94
Age:	At least 2 years
Type:	Straight
Style:	Rye
Mash Bill:	60% rye, 27% malted rye, 13% corn
Color:	Straw
Price:	$$$$

Mike

Nose: Rye grass and ripe plums with a little vanilla and oak.

Taste: Rye grass, plums, and baking spice – cinnamon, allspice – with a little oak.

Finish: Long and dry with oak and cinnamon.

Susan

Nose: Rye grass, vanilla custard, and some fruit.

Taste: Rye grass with some poached pear and a ash of cinnamon.

Finish: Definitely peppery, drying to oak.

Notes

One Eight Distillery, Washington, D.C.

My Score

Notes: _____

_____

_____

Appearance (1-5) _____   Nose (1-25) _____

Taste (1-25) _____   Finish (1-25) _____

Complexity (1-10) _____   Overall Impression (1-10) _____

SCORE _____

Driftless Glen Single Barrel Rye

Proof:	96
Age:	Minimum 6 months
Type:	Single Barrel
Style:	Rye
Mash Bill:	75% rye, 25% malted rye
Color:	Straw
Price:	$$$$

Mike

Nose: Rye grass, citrus, and honey with a hint of bananas.

Taste: Rye grass, citrus, mint, and honey.

Finish: Short and dry with oak.

Susan

Nose: Very light. A little vanilla and some sweet oak with some rye grass around the edges.

Taste: Fresh grass clippings and brown sugar with some ripe apple.

Finish: Dries to light, sweet oak.

Notes

Driftless Glen Distillery, Baraboo, Wisconsin. From Batch No. 3.

My Score

Notes: _____

_____

_____

Appearance (1-5) ____   Nose (1-25) ____

Taste (1-25) ____   Finish (1-25) ____

Complexity (1-10) ____   Overall Impression (1-10) ____

SCORE ____

Ezra Brooks Rye

Proof:	90
Age:	24 months
Type:	Straight
Style:	Rye
Mash Bill:	75% rye, 25% malted rye
Color:	Very pale straw
Price:	$$

Mike

Nose: Very light. Vanilla and rye grass with a hint of fruit.

Taste: Vanilla and rye grass with pepper spice.

Finish: Very long and peppery.

Susan

Nose: Very light with some fruit and sugar.

Taste: Spiced peaches. Very light. Not hot.

Finish: Very short. Some mild pepper.

Notes

Sourced by Luxco of St. Louis, Missouri from MGP in Lawrenceburg, Indiana.

My Score

Notes: _____

_____

_____

Appearance (1-5) _____   Nose (1-25) _____

Taste (1-25) _____   Finish (1-25) _____

Complexity (1-10) _____   Overall Impression (1-10) _____

SCORE _____

F.E.W. Rye

Proof:	93
Age:	Less than 4 years
Type:	Not straight
Style:	Rye
Mash Bill:	70% rye, 20% corn, 10% malted rye
Color:	Dark Straw
Price:	$$$$$

Mike

Nose: Cotton candy spicy with nutmeg and cinnamon.

Taste: Brown sugar and baking spices, like a Christmas cookie with a hint of dates and apricots.

Finish: Dry with oak and spice.

Susan

Nose: Vanilla and green apples underlie lots of rye grass and sweet spice.

Taste: Rye spice with sweet underpinning from the corn in the mash bill. Nutmeg with apples and new leather.

Finish: Medium and warm with no bitterness.

Notes

F.E.W. Spirits, Evanston, Illinois. First distillery in Evanston, ever, since the town was founded by Methodists as a haven of temperance from the evils of whiskey-soaked Chicago. This is a very enjoyable sipping rye that would make a fine Manhattan.

My Score

Notes: _____

_____

_____

Appearance (1-5) ____   Nose (1-25) ____

Taste (1-25) ____   Finish (1-25) ____

Complexity (1-10) ____   Overall Impression (1-10) ____

SCORE ____

Five Fathers Rye

Proof:	110
Age:	NAS
Type:	Not straight
Style:	Rye
Mash Bill:	100% malted rye
Color:	Very Pale Straw
Price:	$$$$ (375 mL)

Mike

Nose:	Rye grass and cereal malt with a hint of vanilla and spice.
Taste:	Very Scotch-like. Rye grass, cereal malt, and pepper spice with a hint of citrus.
Finish:	Short and spicy.

Susan

Nose:	Lots of rye spice with vanilla and some herbal notes.
Taste:	Rich mouthfeel. Burnt vanilla with lots of rye spice, but it's not hot.
Finish:	Dry spice layers drying to sweet oak.

Notes

Old Pogue Distillery, Maysville, Kentucky. Water softens the spice, but it is perfectly enjoyable sipped neat.

My Score

Notes: _____

_____

_____

Appearance (1-5) _____   Nose (1-25) _____

Taste (1-25) _____   Finish (1-25) _____

Complexity (1-10) _____   Overall Impression (1-10) _____

SCORE _____

Flag Hill Straight Rye Whiskey

Proof:	90
Age:	NAS
Type:	Straight
Style:	Rye
Mash Bill:	85% rye, 15% malted barley
Color:	Very, Very Pale Straw
Price:	$$$$$

Mike

Nose: Rye grass, vanilla, and a hint of orange blossom.

Taste: Exactly matches the nose.

Finish: Medium long and spicy with only a hint of oak.

Susan

Nose: Fresh rye grass with a bit of marmalade on lightly toasted bread.

Taste: Toasted marshmallow with some toffee, dates, and citrus.

Finish: Long and spicy, but not hot.

Notes

Flag Hill Distillery & Winery, Lee, New Hampshire. First legal distillery in New Hampshire since Prohibition. The rye is grown on the farm.

My Score

Notes: _____

_____

_____

Appearance (1-5) _____   Nose (1-25) _____

Taste (1-25) _____   Finish (1-25) _____

Complexity (1-10) _____   Overall Impression (1-10) _____

SCORE _____

Founder's Rye Whiskey

Proof: 90
Age: 1 year
Type: Small Batch
Style: Rye
Mash Bill: Not released
Color: Pale Straw
Price: $$$$

Mike

Nose: Rye grass, vanilla, and a hint of cherries.
Taste: Rye grass, cherries, a little vanilla, and baking spices.
Finish: Medium long with oak and baking spices.

Susan

Nose: Lots of rye grass and brown sugar with a bit of vanilla and baking spice.
Taste: Rye crisp, some cherries, and light pepper spice.
Finish: Ends with a dash of pepper.

Notes

Taconic Distillery, Stanfordville, New York. Grain and spring water used in distillation from the Hudson River Valley.

My Score		
Notes: _____		
_____		
_____		
Appearance (1-5) ____	Nose (1-25) ____	
Taste (1-25) ____	Finish (1-25) ____	
Complexity (1-10) ____	Overall Impression (1-10) ____	
SCORE ____		

George Dickel Rye

Proof:	90
Age:	NAS
Type:	Not straight
Style:	Rye
Mash Bill:	95% rye, 5% malted barley
Color:	Light Straw
Price:	$$

Mike

Nose: Rye grass and smoke with some oak and spice.

Taste: Rye grass, vanilla, a bit of spearmint, and oak.

Finish: Dry with oak and mint.

Susan

Nose: Rye cereal, straw, some mint.

Taste: Rye crisp, bran flakes. Not complex.

Finish: Short with a little smoke and mint.

Notes

George Dickel Distillery, Tullahoma, Tennessee. Distilled at MGP in Lawrenceburg, Indiana, but filtered through sugar maple charcoal and aged in Tennessee.

My Score

Notes: _____

_____

_____

Appearance (1-5) _____ Nose (1-25) _____

Taste (1-25) _____ Finish (1-25) _____

Complexity (1-10) _____ Overall Impression (1-10) _____

SCORE _____

George Remus Rye

Proof:	93.3
Age:	Over 3 years
Type:	Small Batch
Style:	Rye
Mash Bill:	100% local rye
Color:	Very, Very Pale Straw
Price:	$$$

Mike

Nose: Young whiskey. Rye grass and a hint of citrus.

Taste: Rye grass, vanilla, with a hint of citrus and spice.

Finish: Long and spicy.

Susan

Nose: Suggestion of rye grass and spice. Simple.

Taste: Arugula salad sprinkled with caraway seeds. Some citrus.

Finish: Pepper and oak.

Notes

Bottled by Queen City Whiskey, Bardstown, Kentucky. Distilled at MGP, Lawrenceburg, Indiana. George Remus was a notorious bootlegger in Cincinnati (nick named The Queen City) during Prohibition.

My Score

Notes: _____

_____

_____

Appearance (1-5) ____	Nose (1-25) ____	
Taste (1-25) ____	Finish (1-25) ____	
Complexity (1-10) ____	Overall Impression (1-10) ____	

SCORE ____

George Washington's Straight Rye

Proof:	86
Age:	4 years
Type:	Straight
Style:	Rye
Mash Bill:	60% rye, 35% corn, 5% malted barley
Color:	Straw
Price:	$$$$$ (375 mL)

Mike

Nose: Ripe apples and pears, vanilla, and only a hint of oak.

Taste: Apples, pears and a hint of berries with vanilla, baking spices and a little oak and leather. Very brandy-like.

Finish: Very long. Starts fruity, but slowly dries to oak.

Susan

Nose: Herbal with burnt candle and fruit.

Taste: Smoky with tobacco and leather followed by apples and vanilla. A drop of water brings out berries and pears.

Finish: Long and smoky, almost like a peated Scotch.

Notes

George Washington Distillery, Mt. Vernon, Virginia. Recreation of the first president's distillery with a copper pot still heated by wood fire. Yearly limited editions vary. This was the 2017 release. Only available at the distillery.

My Score		
Notes: _____		
_____		
_____		
Appearance (1-5) ____	Nose (1-25) ____	
Taste (1-25) ____	Finish (1-25) ____	
Complexity (1-10) ____	Overall Impression (1-10) ____	
SCORE ____		

George Washington's Unaged Rye

Proof:	86
Age:	Not aged
Type:	New make
Style:	Rye
Mash Bill:	60% rye, 35% corn, 5% malted barley
Color:	Clear
Price:	$$$$$ (375 mL)

Mike

Nose: Rye grass, pepper, and a very small hint of fruit.

Taste: Rye grass, corn, and pepper with a hint of pears. Nice mouthfeel.

Finish: Long and peppery.

Susan

Nose: Spicy rye and a bit of dried fruit.

Taste: Marbled rye bread.

Finish: Surprisingly sweet with some peppery spice.

Notes

George Washington Distillery, Mt. Vernon, Virginia. Re-creation of the first president's distillery (est. 1797) with a copper pot still heated by wood fire. Yearly limited editions vary. This was a 2018 release. Only available at the distillery.

My Score

Notes: _____

_____

_____

Appearance (1-5)	____	Nose (1-25)	____
Taste (1-25)	____	Finish (1-25)	____
Complexity (1-10)	____	Overall Impression (1-10)	____

SCORE ____

Greenhat Rye

Proof:	90
Age:	3 years
Type:	Straight, Single Barrel
Style:	Rye
Mash Bill:	73% Maryland rye, 27% distiller's and brewer's malt
Color:	Light Straw
Price:	$$$$$

Mike

Nose: Malt, rye grass, vanilla, and a hint of apples.

Taste: Green apple, malt, rye grass, vanilla, and baking spice.

Finish: Medium long with some oak and spice.

Susan

Nose: Lots of malt followed by rye grass, apples, and caramel.

Taste: Rye grass and baking spice with nuts, caramel and some fruit.

Finish: Long and nutty with malt, ending in rye spice.

Notes

New Columbia Distillers, LLC, Washington, D.C. Pot distilled. Uses English and American ale styles of yeast. Think of beer and a shot in one glass.

My Score

Notes: _____

_____

_____

Appearance (1-5) _____   Nose (1-25) _____

Taste (1-25) _____   Finish (1-25) _____

Complexity (1-10) _____   Overall Impression (1-10) _____

SCORE _____

Gun Fighter American Rye Whiskey

Proof:	100
Age:	NAS
Type:	Finished
Style:	Rye
Mash Bill:	60% rye, 34% corn, 6% malted barley
Color:	Light Smber
Price:	$$$

Mike
Nose: Rye grass, apricots, vanilla, and a bit of oak.
Taste: Rye grass, apricots, caramel, and pepper spice.
Finish: Long and dry with oak and pepper.

Susan
Nose: Dark cherries, caramel, baking spices, and some sweet oak.
Taste: Dark fruit and caramel with some nutmeg and a squeeze of citrus.
Finish: Long and figgy. Very pleasant sip.

Notes
Golden Moon Distillery, Golden, Colorado. Aged for at least six months and then finished in French oak port barrels.

My Score

Notes: _____

_____

_____

Appearance (1-5) ____	Nose (1-25)	____
Taste (1-25) ____	Finish (1-25)	____
Complexity (1-10) ____	Overall Impression (1-10)	____
	SCORE ____	

Heaven's Door Rye

Proof: 92
Age: NAS
Type: Straight, Finished
Style: Rye
Mash Bill: Not revealed
Color: Light Straw
Price: $$$$$

Mike
Nose: Lots of citrus – lemon zest, oranges – with vanilla and rye grass.
Taste: Rye grass, lemon peel, baking spices, and oak.
Finish: Medium long with citrus and spice.

Susan
Nose: Very light. Some faint tobacco and rye spice.
Taste: Light, sweet mint with a bit of apples/cherries, coriander, and pepper.
Finish: Starts sweet and dries to oak.

Notes
Heaven's Door Spirits, Columbia, Tennessee. Developed with musician and Nobel Laureate, Bob Dylan. The label is from a design from one of the iron gates Dylan makes in his ironworks studio. Aged in ex-cigar barrels.

My Score

Notes: _____

_____

_____

Appearance (1-5) _____   Nose (1-25) _____
Taste (1-25) _____   Finish (1-25) _____
Complexity (1-10) _____   Overall Impression (1-10) _____
SCORE _____

High West Double Rye

Proof:	90
Age:	NAS
Type:	Straight
Style:	Rye
Mash Bill:	Not available
Color:	Very Pale Straw
Price:	$$$

Mike
Nose: Rye grass, brown sugar, and oak. Very simple nose.

Taste: Rye grass, brown sugar, pepper spice, and a hint of oak.

Finish: Long and spicy with pepper and oak.

Susan
Nose: String herbal rye grass and lashings of cinnamon.

Taste: Very spicy. Lots of cinnamon and a sprinkle of cloves over a caramel base.

Finish: Long and peppery.

Notes
High West Distillery, Park City, Utah. A blend of High West's 2-year rye with a sourced 16-year-old rye.

My Score

Notes: _____

_____

_____

Appearance (1-5) _____   Nose (1-25) _____

Taste (1-25) _____   Finish (1-25) _____

Complexity (1-10) _____   Overall Impression (1-10) _____

SCORE _____

Highspire Rye Whiskey

Proof: 80
Age: < 4 years
Type: Finished
Style: Rye
Mash Bill: 95% rye, 5% malted rye
Color: Pale Straw
Price: $$$$

Mike

Nose: Rye grass, yeast, a light fruit – grapes or raisins.
Taste: Rye grass, grapes, and baking spices with a hint of vanilla.
Finish: Short. Fruity and spicy.

Susan

Nose: Strong rye grass with some sweet mint and vanilla.
Taste: Rye Krisp crackers with some peppery spice and vanilla.
Finish: Lingering rye.

Notes

Kindred Distilled Spirits, Crestwood, Kentucky. Finished in California wine barrels. Goes very well with a cigar.

My Score

Notes: _____

_____

_____

Appearance (1-5) ____   Nose (1-25) ____
Taste (1-25) ____   Finish (1-25) ____
Complexity (1-10) ____   Overall Impression (1-10) ____
SCORE ____

Jack Daniel's Tennessee Straight Rye

Proof: 90
Age: NAS
Type: Straight
Style: Rye
Mash Bill: 70% rye, 18% corn, 12% malted barley
Color: Pale Straw
Price: $$$

Mike

Nose: Rye grass, bananas, smoke, and oak.
Taste: Rye grass, bananas, smoke, and baking spices.
Finish: Very light with oak and spice.

Susan

Nose: Rye grass, some caramel, rye spice.
Taste: Rye crackers dominate with a little caramel, some apples, and pepper.
Finish: Warm and peppery.

Notes

Jack Daniel's Distillery, Lynchburg, Tennessee.

My Score

Notes: _____

_____

_____

Appearance (1-5) _____   Nose (1-25) _____

Taste (1-25) _____   Finish (1-25) _____

Complexity (1-10) _____   Overall Impression (1-10) _____

SCORE _____

James E. Pepper 1776 Straight Rye

Proof:	100
Age:	2 years
Type:	Straight, Non-Chill Filtered
Style:	Rye
Mash Bill:	95% rye, 5% malted barley
Color:	Very Pale Straw
Price:	$$

Mike
Nose: Very light. Vanilla and rye grass and a hint of fruit and corn.
Taste: Vanilla and fruit with rye grass and pepper.
Finish: Very spicy. Pepper with a hint of oak.

Susan
Nose: Herbal with sweet mint notes.
Taste: Caramel, brown sugar, light pepper, dash of coconut, of all things!
Finish: Short, with oak.

Notes
James E. Pepper Distillery, Lexington, Kentucky. Currently sourced from MGP in Lawrenceburg, Indiana.

My Score

Notes: _____

_____

_____

Appearance (1-5)	____	Nose (1-25)	____
Taste (1-25)	____	Finish (1-25)	____
Complexity (1-10)	____	Overall Impression (1-10)	____

SCORE ____

James Oliver Rye

Proof:	100
Age:	2 years
Type:	Not straight
Style:	Rye
Mash Bill:	Unknown
Color:	Very Pale Straw
Price:	$$$

Mike

Nose: Rye grass, fruit, and roses.

Taste: Rye grass, berries and peaches, with oak and spice.

Finish: Short and sweet.

Susan

Nose: Vanilla and some caramel. Some light fruit.

Taste: Vanilla, caramel, and some cherries.

Finish: Dry and spicy.

Notes

Indio Spirits, Portland, Oregon.

My Score

Notes: _____

_____

_____

Appearance (1-5) ____		Nose (1-25) ____
Taste (1-25) ____		Finish (1-25) ____
Complexity (1-10) ____		Overall Impression (1-10) ____
	SCORE ____	

Jefferson's Rye

Proof:	94
Age:	10 years
Type:	Straight
Style:	Rye
Mash Bill:	Unknown
Color:	Straw
Price:	$$$

Mike

Nose: Rye grass, vanilla, and oak.

Taste: Rye grass, caramel, baking spices, and apples.

Finish: Long and dry with oak and pepper spice.

Susan

Nose: Lots of rye spice with some caramel and cinnamon.

Taste: Caramel and raisins with rye spice, white pepper, and nuts.

Finish: Very dry with lots of oak.

Notes

Kentucky Artisans Distillers, LaGrange, Kentucky. Sourced from Canada from the same distillery that supplies Whistle Pig at a fraction the price. Batch 37, bottle 1096.

My Score

Notes: _____

_____

_____

Appearance (1-5) ____	Nose (1-25)	____
Taste (1-25) ____	Finish (1-25)	____
Complexity (1-10) ____	Overall Impression (1-10)	____
	SCORE ____	

Jim Beam Pre-Prohibition Style Rye Whiskey

Proof:	80
Age:	NAS
Type:	Straight
Style:	Rye
Mash Bill:	~51% rye, balance corn and malted barley
Color:	Very Pale Straw
Price:	$$

Mike

Nose: Very light. Rye grass, vanilla, and a hint of spice.

Taste: Vanilla and berries with a little rye grass and oak.

Finish: Dry with oak and pepper spices.

Susan

Nose: Light grain, slightly floral, and sweet pepper.

Taste: Cereal and spices. Quite light.

Finish: Peppery and seems hot for 80 proof.

Notes

Jim Beam Distillery, Clermont, Kentucky. Mash bill not revealed, but from the taste, this is probably just barely rye by law and it will not scare any bourbon drinkers.

My Score

Notes: _____

_____

_____

Appearance (1-5) ____	Nose (1-25)	____
Taste (1-25) ____	Finish (1-25)	____
Complexity (1-10) ____	Overall Impression (1-10)	____
	SCORE ____	

Jim Beam (rī)[1] Straight Rye Whiskey

Proof:	92
Age:	NAS
Type:	Straight
Style:	Rye
Mash Bill:	~51% rye, balance corn and malted barley
Color:	Straw
Price:	$$$$

Mike

Nose: Very light nose. Vanilla and rye grass.

Taste: Light vanilla, rye grass, baking spice, and a hint of oak.

Finish: Dry. The oak comes out in the finish.

Susan

Nose: Some cinnamon and vanilla, but extremely light.

Taste: Sweet corn, with a tiny bit of honey and vanilla. Simple.

Finish: Short with flash of sweetness before the peppery ending.

Notes

Jim Beam Distillery, Clermont, Kentucky. Not much flavor – brown vodka.

My Score

Notes: _____

_____

_____

Appearance (1-5)	____	Nose (1-25)	____
Taste (1-25)	____	Finish (1-25)	____
Complexity (1-10)	____	Overall Impression (1-10)	____

SCORE ____

John Drew Rye

Proof:	90
Age:	NAS, see comments
Type:	Not straight
Style:	Rye
Mash Bill:	Unknown
Color:	Very, Very Pale Straw
Price:	$$$$

Mike

Nose: Rye grass and butterscotch; very little else.

Taste: Rye grass and butterscotch sweetness with just a hint of baking spices.

Finish: Medium long. Starts sweet and gets a little bit spicy.

Susan

Nose: Musty, with some tobacco smoke.

Taste: Tobacco, leather, some caramel candy.

Finish: Sweet oak with some lingering fruit like cough syrup.

Notes

Sourced from Alberta, Canada by John Drew Brands, Auburndale, Florida. Aged in Canada for four years before shipping to Florida for an additional three years of aging. Was caramel coloring added? The sweetness suggests "Yes".

My Score

Notes: _____

_____

_____

Appearance (1-5) _____   Nose (1-25) _____

Taste (1-25) _____   Finish (1-25) _____

Complexity (1-10) _____   Overall Impression (1-10) _____

SCORE _____

Kentucky Owl Kentucky Straight Rye

Proof:	110.6
Age:	11 years
Type:	Straight
Style:	Rye
Mash Bill:	Unknown
Color:	Light Amber
Price:	$$$$$$

Mike

Nose: Dates and prunes, old leather and baking spices with just a hint of rye grass.

Taste: Very brandy-like with berries and dates. There's also leather, tobacco, nutmeg, and allspice.

Finish: Long. Starts sweet and fruity, but dries out with oak and spice.

Susan

Nose: Rich vanilla, dark fruit, sweet spice, and book leather.

Taste: Herbal rye note right up front with vanilla, smoked meat, and baked fruit and spice. Very complex. Water release rich toffee.

Finish: Long and spicy with lots of black pepper. Sweetened by water.

Notes

Sourced by Kentucky Owl, LLC, Bardstown, Kentucky. Proprietor Dixon Dedman (whose great-great grandfather founded the brand) selects premium barrels for his blends. This is a great rye that proves sourcing whiskey can be a good thing. Very limited release, but a unicorn worth chasing.

My Score	
Notes: _____	
_____	
_____	
Appearance (1-5) ____	Nose (1-25) ____
Taste (1-25) ____	Finish (1-25) ____
Complexity (1-10) ____	Overall Impression (1-10) ____
SCORE ____	

Kings County Empire Rye

Proof:	102
Age:	2 years
Type:	Straight
Style:	Rye
Mash Bill:	See notes
Color:	Amber
Price:	$$$$$ (375 mL)

Mike

Nose:	Rye grass and a hint of chocolate with dates and cherries.
Taste:	Rye grass, chocolate covered cherries, vanilla cream, cinnamon, and oak.
Finish:	Long and spicy.

Susan

Nose:	Caramel, pepper, rye grass, hint of spice.
Taste:	Mouthful of baking spice, vanilla, and oak with dried fruit and some chocolate.
Finish:	Long and spicy. Starts sweet and dries pleasantly.

Notes

Kings County Distillery, Brooklyn, New York. 80% New York-grown Dranko rye and 20% English barley malt.

My Score

Notes: _____

_____

_____

Appearance (1-5)	_____	Nose (1-25)	_____
Taste (1-25)	_____	Finish (1-25)	_____
Complexity (1-10)	_____	Overall Impression (1-10)	_____

SCORE _____

Knob Creek Cask Strength Rye

Proof:	119.6
Age:	NAS
Type:	Straight
Style:	Rye
Mash Bill:	Unknown
Color:	Light Amber
Price:	$$$$$

Mike

Nose: Rye grass, vanilla, dark fruit, spice, and oak.

Taste: Rye grass, caramel, pepper spice, tobacco and leather, with a hint of pitted fruit.

Finish: Long and dry with oak and pepper.

Susan

Nose: Cola, caramel, some dark fruit. Sweet for a rye.

Taste: Caramel and cinnamon with some leather and a bit of rye grass.

Finish: Peppery and dry.

Notes

Jim Beam Distillery, Clermont, Kentucky. Better with some water. Less pepper and more fruit. 2018 limited release. Look for it in whiskey bars.

My Score

Notes: _____

_____

_____

Appearance (1-5) _____   Nose (1-25) _____

Taste (1-25) _____   Finish (1-25) _____

Complexity (1-10) _____   Overall Impression (1-10) _____

SCORE _____

Knob Creek Rye Whiskey

Proof:	100
Age:	NAS
Type:	Straight, Small Batch
Style:	Rye
Mash Bill:	Unknown
Color:	Straw
Price:	$$$$$

Mike

Nose:	Rye grass, vanilla, and oak.
Taste:	A bit thin for 100 proof, but nice flavor with vanilla, rye grass, and baking spices.
Finish:	Long and dry with oak and spice.

Susan

Nose:	Vanilla, caramel, and a little honey, plus rye spice.
Taste:	Spicy holiday potpourri with cinnamon and citrus.
Finish:	Sweet spices dry to a dash of pepper.

Notes

Jim Bean Distillery, Clermont, Kentucky. This would be perfect to enjoy by the fireplace with a book.

My Score

Notes: _____

_____

_____

Appearance (1-5) ____   Nose (1-25) ____

Taste (1-25) ____   Finish (1-25) ____

Complexity (1-10) ____   Overall Impression (1-10) ____

SCORE ____

Knob Creek Twice Barreled Rye

Proof: 100
Age: NAS
Type: Straight, Small Batch
Style: Rye
Mash Bill: Unknown
Color: Dark Straw
Price: $$$$

Mike

Nose: Rye grass and caramel with hints of milk chocolate.

Taste: Rye grass, caramel, apples, pepper, and oak.

Finish: Long, dry, and peppery.

Susan

Nose: Rye grass, caramel, ripe cherries.

Taste: Sweet mint, caramel, a little milk chocolate, and dried fruit.

Finish: Dries to peppery, oaky tannins.

Notes

Jim Bean Distillery, Clermont, Kentucky. After initial aging, the whiskey is put in a second, new, deeply charred white oak barrel.

My Score		
Notes: _____		
_____		
_____		
Appearance (1-5) ____	Nose (1-25)	____
Taste (1-25) ____	Finish (1-25)	____
Complexity (1-10) ____	Overall Impression (1-10)	____
SCORE ____		

Lazy Guy 5ᵗʰ Article Rye

Proof:	100
Age:	At least 8 months
Type:	Not straight
Style:	Rye
Mash Bill:	Unknown
Color:	Straw
Price:	$$$$

Mike
Nose: Rye grass, ripe apricots, vanilla.

Taste: Rye grass, apricots, chocolate, and white pepper.

Finish: Long and chocolaty with a hint of oak and spice.

Susan
Nose: Rye spice and jalapeno peppers.

Taste: More jalapeno with rye spice. Suggestion of figs.

Finish: Pepper persists.

Notes
Lazy Guy Distillery, Kennesaw, Georgia. The 5th Article of Incorporation of the town of Kennesaw in 1887 was the license to sell liquor.

My Score

Notes: _____

_____

_____

Appearance (1-5) ـ____   Nose (1-25) ـ____

Taste (1-25) ـ____   Finish (1-25) ـ____

Complexity (1-10) ـ____   Overall Impression (1-10) ـ____

SCORE ـ____

Leadslingers Fighting Spirit Rye

Proof:	90
Age:	NAS
Type:	Not straight
Style:	Rye
Mash Bill:	Unknown
Color:	Straw
Price:	$$$$

Mike

Nose: Rye grass, vanilla with a hint of orange.

Taste: Very thin. Rye grass, vanilla, and a hint of spice.

Finish: Medium long with a hint of spice.

Susan

Nose: Rye grass, a little caramel, dark fruit.

Taste: Dark caramel, brown sugar, rye spices, and dates.

Finish: Light black pepper. Dry.

Notes

Scissortail Distillery, Moore, Oklahoma.

My Score

Notes: _____

_____

_____

Appearance (1-5) _____   Nose (1-25) _____

Taste (1-25) _____   Finish (1-25) _____

Complexity (1-10) _____   Overall Impression (1-10) _____

SCORE _____

Limestone Branch 100% Malted Rye

Proof: 94
Age: 27 months
Type: Limited Edition
Style: Rye
Mash Bill: 100% malted rye
Color: Dark Straw
Price: $$ (375 mL)

Mike
Nose: Rye grass, berries, and a little oak.
Taste: Rye grass, berries, spearmint, with lots of pepper spice and oak.
Finish: Long and spicy.

Susan
Nose: Vanilla, pears, and some newly mown grass.
Taste: Lots of pear on the palate followed by sweet herbs and some black pepper.
Finish: Dries to sweet oak.

Notes
Limestone Branch Distillery, Lebanon, Kentucky. One in the distillery's series of experimental whiskeys. Always worth trying.

My Score

Notes: _____

_____

_____

Appearance (1-5) _____   Nose (1-25) _____

Taste (1-25) _____   Finish (1-25) _____

Complexity (1-10) _____   Overall Impression (1-10) _____

SCORE _____

Lion's Pride Organic Rye

Proof:	80
Age:	NAS
Type:	Single Barrel
Style:	Rye
Mash Bill:	100% rye
Color:	Yellow tint
Price:	$$$$$

Mike

Nose: Bananas and vanilla with a hint of rye grass.

Taste: Rye grass, a hint of banana and black pepper. Very thin mouthfeel.

Finish: Short and grassy.

Susan

Nose: Cellulose tape, rye spice, perhaps some melon and vanilla.

Taste: Lots of rye spice with some surprising fruitiness on the sides of the tongue.

Finish: Short.

Notes

KOVAL Distillery, Chicago. Organic and Kosher.

My Score

Notes: _____

_____

_____

Appearance (1-5)	____	Nose (1-25)	____
Taste (1-25)	____	Finish (1-25)	____
Complexity (1-10)	____	Overall Impression (1-10)	____

SCORE ____

MB Roland Straight Rye

Proof:	107.6
Age:	2 years
Type:	Straight
Style:	Rye
Mash Bill:	68% rye, 27% white corn, 5% malted barley
Color:	Dark Straw
Price:	$$$$

Mike
Nose: Rye grass, French vanilla with some berries and apricots.
Taste: Rye grass, vanilla, cinnamon spice, apricots, and oak.
Finish: Long and spicy with cinnamon and oak.

Susan
Nose: Rye crackers, cinnamon, milk chocolate, berries.
Taste: Caramel apples with some saddle leather and more rye crackers.
Finish: Starts intriguingly sweet and dries to the leather.

Notes
MB Roland Distillery, Pembroke, Kentucky. Uses #4 char barrels. Very unusual rye given the mash bill. Also happens to be highly enjoyable.

My Score

Notes: _____

_____

_____

Appearance (1-5) _____   Nose (1-25) _____

Taste (1-25) _____   Finish (1-25) _____

Complexity (1-10) _____   Overall Impression (1-10) _____

SCORE _____

McKenzie Straight Rye

Proof:	91
Age:	NAS
Type:	Finished
Style:	Rye
Mash Bill:	80% rye 5% malted barley
Color:	Light Straw
Price:	$$$

Mike

Nose: Rye grass and orange blossoms.

Taste: Rye grass, orange blossoms, honey, and baking spices.

Finish: Long and spicy with oak and baking spices.

Susan

Nose: Rye grass, some caramel, and citrus.

Taste: Cereal and rye spice in almost equal measure. Nicely balanced sip with some sweet spice and fruit, too.

Finish: Lingers on the tongue with citrus and honey.

Notes

Finger Lakes Distilling, Burdett, New York. Aged at least 2 years in quarter cask (15 gallon) new charred white oak barrels, then finished in local winery sherry barrels for 2-3 months.

My Score

Notes: _____

_____

_____

Appearance (1-5) _____   Nose (1-25) _____

Taste (1-25) _____   Finish (1-25) _____

Complexity (1-10) _____   Overall Impression (1-10) _____

SCORE _____

Michter's 10-Year Single Barrel Rye

Proof:	92.8
Age:	10 years
Type:	Single Barrel
Style:	Rye
Mash Bill:	Not disclosed
Color:	Straw
Price:	$$$$$$

Mike

Nose: Cherries and berries, caramel, baking spices, and oak.

Taste: Rye grass, cherries and dates, honey and caramel, with nutmeg, cinnamon, and oak.

Finish: Long and dry with baking spices and oak.

Susan

Nose: Strong fresh vegetable note, like a farmers' market. Also, tobacco and vanilla.

Taste: Herbs and spices with undertones of horehound and brown sugar.

Finish: Very dry with oak and pepper.

Notes

Michter's Distillery, Louisville, Kentucky. If you can find it, buy it.

My Score

Notes: _____

_____

_____

Appearance (1-5) ____ Nose (1-25) ____

Taste (1-25) ____ Finish (1-25) ____

Complexity (1-10) ____ Overall Impression (1-10) ____

SCORE ____

Michter's Barrel Strength Rye

Proof:	109.6
Age:	NAS
Type:	Straight, Barrel Strength, Limited Release
Style:	Rye
Mash Bill:	Not released
Color:	Dark Straw
Price:	$$$$$$

Mike

Nose: Rye grass, caramel, and chocolate with some baking spices and oak.

Taste: Citrus fruit, caramel, chocolate, nutmeg, cinnamon and a hint of oak tannins.

Finish: Long. Starts sweet but dries out with spice and oak.

Susan

Nose: Dark toffee, bitter cherries, sorghum, and rye spice.

Taste: Burnt sorghum and new leather. Water releases notes of dark fruit and baking spices.

Finish: Long and smooth drying to sweet oak and pepper.

Notes

Michter's Distillery, Louisville, Kentucky. Another masterpiece from Michter's.

My Score

Notes: _____

_____

_____

Appearance (1-5)	____	Nose (1-25)	____
Taste (1-25)	____	Finish (1-25)	____
Complexity (1-10)	____	Overall Impression (1-10)	____

SCORE ____

Michter's Single Barrel 25-Year Old Rye

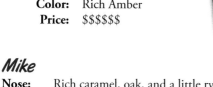

Proof:	117.3
Age:	25 years
Type:	Extra Aged, Single Barrel
Style:	Rye
Mash Bill:	Not disclosed
Color:	Rich Amber
Price:	$$$$$$

Mike

Nose: Rich caramel, oak, and a little rye grass. Water brings out chocolate.

Taste: Rich caramel and oak with some cinnamon spice and citrus fruit. Water brings out some chocolate, more fruit, and baking spices.

Finish: Long, dry, and oaky. Water adds some spice notes.

Susan

Nose: Rich herbal essence, some tobacco, dark fruit, and cinnamon dusted toffee.

Taste: Toffee, fruit cake, whisper of caraway, some herbal spices, and new leather.

Finish: Long and dry with loads of oak.

Notes

Michter's Distillery, Louisville, Kentucky. Probably your best chance to taste this is in a well-stocked whiskey bar. You will pay a premium. It will be worth it.

My Score

Notes: _____

_____

_____

Appearance (1-5) _____   Nose (1-25) _____

Taste (1-25) _____   Finish (1-25) _____

Complexity (1-10) _____   Overall Impression (1-10) _____

SCORE _____

Michter's Toasted Barrel Finished Straight Rye

Proof:	110
Age:	NAS
Type:	Straight, Barrel Strength, Finished, Limited Release
Style:	Rye
Mash Bill:	Not released
Color:	Straw
Price:	$$$$$$

Mike

Nose: Chocolate and caramel with a little citrus fruit and baking spices.

Taste: Citrus and dark chocolate with baking spices – lots of cinnamon – and oak tannins.

Finish: Long and dry with spices and oak.

Susan

Nose: Caramel, rye grass, dates.

Taste: Brown sugar, crème brulee, dark cherries, chocolate. Water smooths it without diminishing flavors.

Finish: Dry and warm.

Notes

Michter's Distillery, Louisville, Kentucky. Wish this one was not such a unicorn!

My Score

Notes: _____

_____

_____

Appearance (1-5)	____	Nose (1-25)	____
Taste (1-25)	____	Finish (1-25)	____
Complexity (1-10)	____	Overall Impression (1-10)	____

SCORE ____

Michter's US★1 Straight Rye

Proof:	84.8
Age:	NAS
Type:	Straight
Style:	Rye
Mash Bill:	Not disclosed
Color:	Straw
Price:	$$$$

Mike

Nose: Rye grass, caramel, baking spices, and a hint of apples.

Taste: Rye grass, corn sweetness, nutmeg and cinnamon with some apples and pears.

Finish: Long and dry with oak and spices.

Susan

Nose: Vanilla and cherry cola. I could nose this all day! Luscious.

Taste: More cherry cola, brown sugar, some chocolate notes and a spine of rye spice.

Finish: Warm and dry with oak and pepper

Notes

Michter's Distillery, Louisville, Kentucky. This rye makes dynamite Manhattans and Sazaracs, if you can bring yourself to mix it.

My Score

Notes: _____

_____

_____

Appearance (1-5) ____	Nose (1-25)	____
Taste (1-25) ____	Finish (1-25)	____
Complexity (1-10) ____	Overall Impression (1-10)	____

SCORE ____

Midwinter Night's Dram

Proof:	98.6
Age:	NAS
Type:	Finished, Non-Chill Filtered
Style:	Rye
Mash Bill:	See notes
Color:	Light Amber
Price:	$$$$$$

Mike

Nose: Rye grass, caramel, baking spices, dark pitted fruit – plums and prunes – with some oak.

Taste: Rye grass and oak up front. The pitted fruit comes mid-palate with some caramel sweetness and baking spices.

Finish: Long, dry, and spicy.

Susan

Nose: Rich caramel, with wine and dark fruit, plus herbal rye spice.

Taste: Cinnamon sprinkled caramel with dark cherries and sweet nuts.

Finish: Long and warm with cinnamon and oak.

Notes

High West Distillery, Park City, Utah. Blend of straight ryes from MGP (Lawrenceburg, Indiana), Barton Distillery (Bardstown, Kentucky) and High West. It's a Christmas pudding in a glass.

My Score

Notes: _____

_____

_____

Appearance (1-5)	____	Nose (1-25) ____
Taste (1-25)	____	Finish (1-25) ____
Complexity (1-10)	____	Overall Impression (1-10) ____

SCORE ____

Minor Case Rye

Proof:	90
Age:	24 months
Type:	Straight, Finished
Style:	Rye
Mash Bill:	Not disclosed
Color:	Light Straw
Price:	$$$$

Mike
Nose: Vanilla and fruit with a light almond note.
Taste: Rye grass, vanilla, berries, and baking spices.
Finish: Medium long with spice and a hint of oak.

Susan
Nose: Light, with whiffs of vanilla and grass.
Taste: More vanilla on the palate with light rye spice.
Finish: Lightly spicy with some oak.

Notes
Limestone Branch Distillery, Lebanon, Kentucky. Sourced from MGP in Lawrenceburg, Indiana and finished in sherry casks in Kentucky.

My Score

Notes: _____

_____

_____

Appearance (1-5)	____	Nose (1-25)	____
Taste (1-25)	____	Finish (1-25)	____
Complexity (1-10)	____	Overall Impression (1-10)	____

SCORE ____

New Riff Kentucky Straight Rye

Proof:	100
Age:	4 years
Type:	Bottled-in-Bond
Style:	Rye
Mash Bill:	95% rye, 5% malted rye
Color:	Straw
Price:	$$$$

Mike

Nose: Rye grass, a hint of brown sugar, and chocolate.

Taste: Rye grass, brown sugar, baking spices, and a hint of berries.

Finish: Long and dry with oak and pepper.

Susan

Nose: Rye grass and vanilla with dark cherries.

Taste: Rye spice and vanilla, plus rich fruitcake.

Finish: Warm and spicy, drying to sweet oak.

Notes

New Riff Distilling, Newport, Kentucky. The bonded stamp says it was distilled in the fall of 2014 and bottled in fall 2018.

My Score

Notes: _____

_____

_____

Appearance (1-5) _____   Nose (1-25) _____

Taste (1-25) _____   Finish (1-25) _____

Complexity (1-10) _____   Overall Impression (1-10) _____

SCORE _____

North Coast Rye

Proof: 90
Age: NAS
Type: Small Batch
Style: Rye
Mash Bill: Rye and malted barley
Color: Straw
Price: $$$$

Mike

Nose: Rye grass, vanilla, and a hint of fruit – peaches and apples.
Taste: Rye grass, honey, and vanilla with pear fruit and oak.
Finish: Medium long with oak and some white pepper.

Susan

Nose: Spicy herbal nose with a whiff of vanilla.
Taste: Pine cone, rye grass, pepper, and cloves.
Finish: Medium long with pepper and tannins.

Notes

Traverse City Whiskey Co., Traverse City, Michigan. Pleasant and very different sip rich with fruit and spices.

My Score	
Notes: _____	
_____	
_____	
Appearance (1-5) ____	Nose (1-25) ____
Taste (1-25) ____	Finish (1-25) ____
Complexity (1-10) ____	Overall Impression (1-10) ____
SCORE ____	

North Fork Rye

Proof: 92
Age: 2 years
Type: Small Batch
Style: Rye
Mash Bill: Rye, rye malt, corn
Color: Straw
Price: $ $ (375 mL)

Mike

Nose: Rye bread dough, raisins, and apricots.
Taste: Rye grass, raisins and apricots, a hint of peaches with baking spices and oak.
Finish: Medium long with oak and spices.

Susan

Nose: Rye bread, some vanilla with nuts and raisins.
Taste: Mellow rye with some toffee and more nuts and raisins.
Finish: Fads fairly quickly, but there is a tantalizing sweet note at the very end.

Notes

Glacier Distilling Company, Coram. Montana. Batch number 18G06.

My Score

Notes: _____

_____

_____

Appearance (1-5) ____   Nose (1-25) ____
Taste (1-25) ____   Finish (1-25) ____
Complexity (1-10) ____   Overall Impression (1-10) ____
SCORE ____

Old Carter Rye

Proof:	112.2
Age:	NAS
Type:	Barrel Proof
Style:	Rye
Mash Bill:	95% rye
Color:	Amber
Price:	$$$$$$

Mike

Nose: Caramel, rye grass, a little apricot. Water opens the nose with more caramel and fruit – pineapple.

Taste: Very tannic. Water reduces the tannins, bringing out the caramel, ripe apples, and baking spices.

Finish: Long with oak and spices. Very dry. Water tames the tannins and makes the finish a little less hot.

Susan

Nose: Sweet nose with rye spice, brown sugar, and fruit salad.

Taste: The rye spice is well balanced with citrus, vanilla, brown sugar, and baking spice. Do add water to lessen the heat and open it.

Finish: Warm and smooth, drying to oak.

Notes

Selected and sourced from MGP in Lawrenceburg, Indiana by Mark and Sherri Carter, who had partnered with Dixon Dedman on Kentucky Owl. This was Bottle 389 of 1269 from Batch 1.

My Score

Notes: _____

_____

_____

Appearance (1-5) _____   Nose (1-25) _____

Taste (1-25) _____   Finish (1-25) _____

Complexity (1-10) _____   Overall Impression (1-10) _____

SCORE _____

Old Forester Rye

Proof:	100
Age:	NAS
Type:	Straight
Style:	Rye
Mash Bill:	65% rye, 20% malted barley, 15% corn
Color:	Light Amber
Price:	$$

Mike

Nose: Rye grass, honey, a little fruit – apples, pears, and bananas.

Taste: Rye grass, caramel, baking spices, a little fruit and oak.

Finish: Long and dry with oak and cinnamon.

Susan

Nose: Bananas and a bit of honey with a spike of herbal spice.

Taste: Much fruiter than most ryes, supported with underlying caramel and herbs.

Finish: Long and spicy.

Notes

Brown-Forman, Louisville, Kentucky. Water amplifies the fruit and smooths the spices.

My Score

Notes: _____

_____

_____

Appearance (1-5) _____   Nose (1-25) _____

Taste (1-25) _____   Finish (1-25) _____

Complexity (1-10) _____   Overall Impression (1-10) _____

SCORE _____

Old Henry Clay Straight Rye Whiskey

Proof:	86
Age:	NAS
Type:	Straight
Style:	Rye
Mash Bill:	> 90% rye
Color:	Pale Straw
Price:	$$

Mike

Nose: Rye grass, apricots, and anise.

Taste: Thin and watery with rye grass, apricots, and liquorice. Would like to try this at 100 proof.

Finish: Short with a hint of oak.

Susan

Nose: Very herbal rye with some anise.

Taste: Tastes just like the nose smells with some addition of figs or dates.

Finish: Spicy, drying to oak tannins.

Notes

James E. Pepper Distillery, Lexington, Kentucky. Currently sourced from MGP, Lawrenceburg, Indiana. With this high rye content, you would never mistake it for bourbon!

My Score

Notes: _____

_____

_____

Appearance (1-5) _____   Nose (1-25) _____

Taste (1-25) _____   Finish (1-25) _____

Complexity (1-10) _____   Overall Impression (1-10) _____

SCORE _____

Old Maysville Club Rye

Proof: 100
Age: At least 4 years
Type: Bottled-in-Bond
Style: Rye
Mash Bill: Unknown
Color: Straw
Price: $$$$$

Mike

Nose: Rye grass, vanilla, malt, and a hint of peaches.
Taste: Rye grass, malt, peaches, and a hint of citrus, baking spice, and oak.
Finish: Long, dry, with oak and spice.

Susan

Nose: Freshly baked rye bread, dark caramel, and some vanilla.
Taste: Rich mouthfeel with notes of caramel and sweet nuts. Water amplifies the nuttiness.
Finish: Long, dry, and peppery.

Notes

Old Pogue Distillery, Maysville, Kentucky. Only two barrels produced per week. Very malty. Scotch and Irish whiskey lovers will like this a lot.

My Score

Notes: _____

_____

_____

Appearance (1-5) _____   Nose (1-25) _____
Taste (1-25) _____   Finish (1-25) _____
Complexity (1-10) _____   Overall Impression (1-10) _____
SCORE _____

Old Overholt Bonded Straight Rye Whiskey

Proof:	100
Age:	At least 4 years
Type:	Bottled-in-Bond
Style:	Rye
Mash Bill:	Unknown
Color:	Pale Straw
Price:	$$

Mike

Nose: Vanilla, dates, rye grass, and a hint of tobacco.
Taste: Vanilla, cherries, pepper spice, and rye grass.
Finish: Dry – oak and pepper spice.

Susan

Nose: Sweet mint, very light apple, tobacco leaf.
Taste: Sweet cereal, touch of mint, light pepper.
Finish: Nice mouthfeel drying to oak.

Notes

Jim Beam Distillery, Clermont, Kentucky. Would make a good Manhattan.

My Score		
Notes: _____		
_____		
_____		
Appearance (1-5) ____	Nose (1-25)	____
Taste (1-25) ____	Finish (1-25)	____
Complexity (1-10) ____	Overall Impression (1-10)	____
SCORE ____		

Old Overholt Rye

Proof:	80
Age:	NAS
Type:	Straight
Style:	Rye
Mash Bill:	Unknown
Color:	Pale Straw
Price:	$$

Mike

Nose: Rye grass, caramel, oak, and a hint of berries.

Taste: Rye grass, caramel, a little baking spice, oak, and berries.

Finish: Light. Short with a hint of oak.

Susan

Nose: Light, with some rye grass and apples.

Taste: Rye bread crust with an herbal note. A little fruit and pepper.

Finish: Warm and dry with some sweet oak.

Notes

Jim Beam Distillery, Clermont, Kentucky. A lot of flavor for 80 proof and under $20 a bottle.

My Score

Notes: _____

_____

_____

Appearance (1-5)	____	Nose (1-25)	____
Taste (1-25)	____	Finish (1-25)	____
Complexity (1-10)	____	Overall Impression (1-10)	____
	SCORE ____		

Old Portreo Straight Rye

Proof:	97
Age:	NAS
Type:	Straight
Style:	Rye
Mash Bill:	100% malted rye
Color:	Pale Straw
Price:	$$$$$

Mike

Nose: Rye grass, prunes and dates, vanilla, a hint of baking spice and oak.

Taste: Rye grass, raisins, dates, and apricots with nutmeg, allspice, and a hint of cinnamon with some oak wood.

Finish: Long, dry, and spicy with a hint of oak.

Susan

Nose: Green apples, rye toast, vanilla custard.

Taste: Vanilla and wood smoke with some cinnamon and sweet oak.

Finish: Long, dry, peppery.

Notes

Anchor Distilling, San Francisco, California. Yes, the Anchor Steam Beer people. Mostly available in California.

My Score

Notes: _____

_____

_____

Appearance (1-5) ____   Nose (1-25) ____

Taste (1-25) ____   Finish (1-25) ____

Complexity (1-10) ____   Overall Impression (1-10) ____

SCORE ____

Old Tahoe Straight Rye

Proof:	86
Age:	3 years
Type:	Straight
Style:	Rye
Mash Bill:	100% rye
Color:	Straw
Price:	$$$$

Mike

Nose: Rye grass and molasses with a hint of pepper.

Taste: Rye grass, molasses, and pepper with a hint of oak.

Finish: Dry and spicy with pepper and oak.

Susan

Nose: Lashings of burnt caramel, with some apricot and pepper.

Taste: Rye cereal with dark fruit, burnt sugar and horehound candy.

Finish: Pleasantly peppery.

Notes

Old Tahoe Distillery, Silver City, Nevada. Batch No. 20. Label states "Bottled for Old Tahoe Distillery, Minden, New York."

My Score

Notes: _____

_____

_____

Appearance (1-5)	____	Nose (1-25)	____
Taste (1-25)	____	Finish (1-25)	____
Complexity (1-10)	____	Overall Impression (1-10)	____

SCORE ____

O.Z. Tyler Rye

Proof:	90
Age:	6 months
Type:	Not straight
Style:	Rye
Mash Bill:	95% rye
Color:	Extremely Pale Straw; Almost Clear
Price:	$$$

Mike

Nose: Rye grass and a hint of oak.

Taste: Rye grass and new make whiskey. Just a hint of oak and vanilla.

Finish: Short. Nothing but alcohol.

Susan

Nose: Lots of rye grain with some faint spice and apples.

Taste: Some vanilla and sweet spice. A little apple. Not complex.

Finish: Lightly spicy, but mainly sweet.

Notes

O.Z. Tyler Distillery, Owensboro, Kentucky. Uses the TerrePURE process to "accelerate" aging. This is like "dry water." The whiskey needs age and there is no substitute for time.

My Score

Notes: _____

_____

_____

Appearance (1-5)	____	Nose (1-25)	____
Taste (1-25)	____	Finish (1-25)	____
Complexity (1-10)	____	Overall Impression (1-10)	____

SCORE ____

Peerless Oak & Pepper Rye

Proof: 108.6
Age: 2 years
Type: Straight, Barrel Proof, Single Barrel
Style: Rye
Mash Bill: Not released
Color: Straw
Price: $$$$$$

Mike
Nose: Rye grass and cereal with some spice and oak.
Taste: Rye grass and caramel/vanilla with some pepper spice and almonds.
Finish: Long, dry, and spicy with white pepper.

Susan
Nose: Maple syrup, banana, and hazelnuts.
Taste: Drier than the nose. Oak and pepper predominate, just as the label promises.
Finish: Dry and spicy.

Notes
Kentucky Peerless Distilling Co., Louisville, Kentucky. Water releases Indian curry spices. Limited edition available at the distillery (and in fine whiskey bars).

My Score

Notes: _____

_____

_____

Appearance (1-5) _____   Nose (1-25) _____

Taste (1-25) _____   Finish (1-25) _____

Complexity (1-10) _____   Overall Impression (1-10) _____

SCORE _____

Peerless Rye Small Batch 2-Year

Proof:	108.5
Age:	2 years
Type:	Straight, Barrel Proof, Small Batch
Style:	Rye
Mash Bill:	Not released
Color:	Pale Straw
Price:	$$$$$$

Mike

Nose: Rye grass, vanilla, ripe peaches, and a hint of baking spice.

Taste: Rye grass, peaches, and pepper with some vanilla and honeysuckle.

Finish: Dry and peppery with a hint of oak.

Susan

Nose: Rye roll with some brown sugar and sweet mint, cinnamon, and new leather.

Taste: Some underlying corn sweetness on the palate, with more brown sugar and vanilla.

Finish: Long and spicy with oak dryness.

Notes

Kentucky Peerless Distilling Co., Louisville, Kentucky. Small batches use 4 to 6 barrels each. Please consider Peerless photos generic. The distillery has had many small releases, as it standardizes its rye. Bottle shape will be the same.

My Score

Notes: _____

_____

_____

Appearance (1-5)	____	Nose (1-25)	____
Taste (1-25)	____	Finish (1-25)	____
Complexity (1-10)	____	Overall Impression (1-10)	____

SCORE ____

Peerless Rye Small Batch 3-Year

Proof:	109.1
Age:	3 years
Type:	Small Batch, Non-Chill Filtered, Sweet Mash
Style:	Rye
Mash Bill:	Not released
Color:	Light Amber
Price:	$$$$$$

Mike

Nose: Rye grass, a little apple and vanilla with a hint of oak. Water brings out a hint of chocolate.

Taste: Rye grass, vanilla, ripe apples and pears, with some oak and pepper spice.

Finish: Long and dry with oak and a hint of pepper.

Susan

Nose: Spicy rye grass, light fruitiness, some baking spices.

Taste: Lots of stewed fruit including apples and prunes with pepper and oak.

Finish: Long and warm with a trace of milk chocolate.

Notes

Kentucky Peerless Distillery, Louisville, Kentucky. Lovely sipping rye even at the high proof. A little water brings out more fruit and chocolate.

My Score

Notes: _____

_____

_____

Appearance (1-5) ____   Nose (1-25) ____

Taste (1-25) ____   Finish (1-25) ____

Complexity (1-10) ____   Overall Impression (1-10) ____

SCORE ____

Peerless Single Barrel

Proof:	108.1
Age:	3 years, 4 months
Type:	Straight, Barrel Proof, Single Barrel
Style:	Rye
Mash Bill:	Not released
Color:	Dark Straw
Price:	$$$$$$

Mike

Nose: Caramel and very ripe plums with a bit of oak and spicy rye grass.

Taste: Rye grass, caramel and very ripe apple, with a hint of honey and oak.

Finish: Medium long and spicy with pepper and oak tempered by ripe apple.

Susan

Nose: Sweet oak with brown sugar and caramel. Just a whiff of fruit and baking spice.

Taste: Rye grass is subtle and quickly turns to cinnamon red hots with some notes of cherry.

Finish: Long and spicy jot in a very pleasant way.

Notes

Kentucky Peerless Distilling Co., Louisville, Kentucky. Water brings out a little more rye and a lot more brown sugar.

My Score

Notes: _____

_____

_____

Appearance (1-5) _____   Nose (1-25) _____

Taste (1-25) _____   Finish (1-25) _____

Complexity (1-10) _____   Overall Impression (1-10) _____

SCORE _____

Pikesville Rye

Proof: 110
Age: 6 years
Type: Barrel Strength
Style: Rye
Mash Bill: Not released
Color: Light Amber
Price: $$$$$

Mike
Nose: Rye grass, caramel, hints of dates and apples.
Taste: Rye grass, caramel, pepper spice, and a hint of dates or cherries.
Finish: Long, dry, with oak and spice.

Susan
Nose: Light vanilla and caramel. Some apricot. Very bourbon-like.
Taste: Some caramel and pungent spice with light rye notes.
Finish: Short and peppery.

Notes
Heaven Hill Distillery, Louisville, Kentucky. Aging and bottling facilities are in Bardstown.

My Score
Notes: _____

_____

_____

Appearance (1-5) _____   Nose (1-25) _____

Taste (1-25) _____   Finish (1-25) _____

Complexity (1-10) _____   Overall Impression (1-10) _____

SCORE _____

Pinhook Bourbon N Rye

Proof:	93.5
Age:	24 months
Type:	Straight
Style:	Rye
Mash bill:	Unknown
Color:	Pale straw
Price:	$$$$

Mike
Nose: Rye grass, berries and dates, a hint of oak.
Taste: Rye grass, vanilla, a little spice and oak with a hint of berries.
Finish: Short with a hint of spice.

Susan
Nose: Rye grass, cellulose, a tiny bit of caramel, and perhaps some berries.
Taste: Very herbal, though not unpleasant. Cinnamon emerges on the center of the tongue.
Finish: Spicy. Quickly dries to oak after initial sweetness.

Notes
Bottled by Peristyle LLC, Frankfort, KY. Distilled at MGP, Lawrenceburg, Indiana. Various rye expressions named after Thoroughbred racehorses, which are depicted on the labels.

My Score

Notes: _____

_____

_____

Appearance (1-5) _____   Nose (1-25) _____

Taste (1-25) _____   Finish (1-25) _____

Complexity (1-10) _____   Overall Impression (1-10) _____

SCORE _____

Pinhook Rye Humor

Proof: 97
Age: 3 years
Type: Straight
Style: Rye
Mash Bill: Unknown
Color: Pale Straw
Price: $$$$

Mike

Nose: Rye grass, mint, vanilla and a hint of spice.
Taste: Rye grass, vanilla, a hint of spearmint and spice.
Finish: Long and minty.

Susan

Nose: Cardamom, caraway, and a whiff of mint.
Taste: Rye grass, Indian spices.
Finish: Dry and spicy.

Notes

Bottled by Peristyle LLC, Frankfort, Kentucky. Distilled at MGP, Lawrenceburg, Indiana. Various rye expressions named after Thoroughbred racehorses, which are depicted on the labels.

My Score

Notes: _____

_____

_____

Appearance (1-5) _____   Nose (1-25) _____

Taste (1-25) _____   Finish (1-25) _____

Complexity (1-10) _____   Overall Impression (1-10) _____

SCORE _____

Rabbit Hole Rye

Proof:	95
Age:	2 years
Type:	Straight
Style:	Rye
Mash Bill:	95% rye, 5% malted barley
Color:	Straw
Price:	$$$$

Mike

Nose: Very light. Rye grass and vanilla.

Taste: Rye grass, vanilla, a bit of apricot or peach, with some baking spice and oak.

Finish: Long and dry with oak and spice.

Susan

Nose: Faint rye grass and dark fruit.

Taste: Rye grass, pepper, with vanilla, raisins, and dates.

Finish: Smooth and spicy.

Notes

Rabbit Hole Distillery, Louisville, Kentucky. Currently sourced from New Riff in Newport, Kentucky, but the Louisville distillery is now in production. Batch 1, bottle 739.

My Score

Notes: _____

_____

_____

Appearance (1-5) _____   Nose (1-25) _____

Taste (1-25) _____   Finish (1-25) _____

Complexity (1-10) _____   Overall Impression (1-10) _____

SCORE _____

Ravenswood Rye

Proof:	90
Age:	NAS
Type:	Organic
Style:	Rye
Mash Bill:	60% rye, 40% wheat
Color:	Straw
Price:	$$$$

Mike

Nose: Apple fruit and rye grass, vanilla, and some baking spice.

Taste: Apple and vanilla with fruit, nutmeg, oak, and rye grass.

Finish: Short and dry. Starts fruity, but quickly dries with oak and spice.

Susan

Nose: Sweet cereal with a beer-like aroma.

Taste: Mild acetone, but more pleasant that that sounds, with some stick candy.

Finish: Very short.

Notes

Journeyman Distillery, Three Oaks, Michigan. Aged in 15 gallon barrels. Batch 32, bottle 54.

My Score

Notes: _____

_____

_____

Appearance (1-5)	____	Nose (1-25)	____
Taste (1-25)	____	Finish (1-25)	____
Complexity (1-10)	____	Overall Impression (1-10)	____
	SCORE ____		

Red-Handed Rye

Proof: 100
Age: 10 years
Type: Not straight
Style: Rye
Mash Bill: 53% rye, 39% corn, 8% malted barley
Color: Very Pale Straw
Price: $$$$$

Mike

Nose: Strawberry Peeps. Marshmallow and fruit.
Taste: Strawberry and vanilla with some baking spice.
Finish: Short and sweet with only the slightest hint of oak.

Susan

Nose: Artificial strawberry with herbal notes.
Taste: Cut grass and sugar sprinkles.
Finish: Short and sweet with pepper at the end.

Notes

Treaty Oak Distilling, Dipping Springs, Texas. Sourced from Kentucky and Virginia and proofed with limestone filtered water from Dipping Springs.

My Score

Notes: _____

_____

_____

Appearance (1-5) _____   Nose (1-25) _____

Taste (1-25) _____   Finish (1-25) _____

Complexity (1-10) _____   Overall Impression (1-10) _____

SCORE _____

Rendezvous Rye

Proof:	92
Age:	NAS
Type:	Straight
Style:	Rye
Mash Bill:	See notes
Color:	Dark Straw
Price:	$$$$$

Mike

Nose: Rye grass, buttered toffee, baking spices, and a little fruit.

Taste: Thin mouthfeel, but tasty. Caramel, rye grass, and spices up front, with some citrus and oak following.

Finish: Long dry, and spicy with oak and cinnamon.

Susan

Nose: Vanilla, light smoke, with some leather and subtle berries.

Taste: Malted barley note predominates, followed by some corn and some smoke, with fruit and nuts.

Finish: Very dry and herbal with oak. Water bring out more fruit.

Notes

High West Distillery, Park City, Utah. Blend of ryes from MGP (95% rye, 5% malted barley) and High West's (80% rye, 20 % malted rye).

My Score

Notes: _____

_____

_____

Appearance (1-5)	____	Nose (1-25)	____
Taste (1-25)	____	Finish (1-25)	____
Complexity (1-10)	____	Overall Impression (1-10)	____

SCORE ____

Revolution Rye

Proof:	96
Age:	At least 1 year
Type:	Not straight
Style:	Rye
Mash Bill:	100% rye
Color:	Straw
Price:	$$$$

Mike
Nose: Rye grass, very ripe peaches with a hint of vanilla.

Taste: Rye grass, peaches, vanilla, and cinnamon.

Finish: Dry with oak and a hint of cinnamon.

Susan
Nose: Rye grass and pepper with some sweet mint.

Taste: Rye grass, cayenne, and autumn leaves.

Finish: Short and peppery. Tingles on the tongue.

Notes
Mad River Distillers, Warren, Vermont. Made with three types of rye, including a malted chocolate rye. Aged in barrels smaller than the standard 53 gallon. Farm-to-glass. Distillery housed in a renovated horse barn.

My Score

Notes: _____

_____

_____

Appearance (1-5) ____   Nose (1-25) ____

Taste (1-25) ____   Finish (1-25) ____

Complexity (1-10) ____   Overall Impression (1-10) ____

SCORE ____

Rittenhouse Bonded Rye

Proof:	100
Age:	NAS
Type:	Bottled-in-Bond
Style:	Rye
Mash Bill:	Not disclosed
Color:	Dark Straw
Price:	$$

Mike

Nose: Caramel and rye grass with corn sweetness and a hint of apples.

Taste: Caramel and white pepper with some rye grass. A hint of apple in the background.

Finish: Long, dry, and spicy. Oak tannins and white pepper.

Susan

Nose: Spiced pears and brown sugar.

Taste: Vanilla, pears, and a dash of nutmeg.

Finish: Lightly oaky and long.

Notes

Heaven Hill Distillery, Louisville, Kentucky. Aging and bottling facilities are in Bardstown. Very reliable cocktail base at a great price.

My Score

Notes: _____

_____

_____

Appearance (1-5) _____   Nose (1-25) _____

Taste (1-25) _____   Finish (1-25) _____

Complexity (1-10) _____   Overall Impression (1-10) _____

SCORE _____

Riverboat Rye

Proof:	80
Age:	Less than 4 years
Type:	Small Batch
Style:	Rye
Mash Bill:	Unknown
Color:	Barely there
Price:	$$

Mike
Nose: Citrus, rye grass, and vanilla. Very young.
Taste: Citrus, rye grass, and pepper spice.
Finish: Long with some oak and lots of pepper.

Susan
Nose: Slightly resinous with some horehound.
Taste: Some rye spice and a little oak and lemon. Very simple.
Finish: Oak lingers.

Notes
Bottled by Bardstown Barrel Selections. Distilled at MGP, Lawrenceburg, Indiana.

My Score
Notes: _____

_____

_____

Appearance (1-5) ____   Nose (1-25) ____

Taste (1-25) ____   Finish (1-25) ____

Complexity (1-10) ____   Overall Impression (1-10) ____

SCORE ____

Roaming Man Tennessee Rye

Proof: 122.2
Age: NAS
Type: Barrel Strength
Style: Rye
Mash Bill: 51% rye, 45% corn, 4% barley
Color: Amber
Price: $$$$ (375 mL)

Mike

Nose: Rye grass and vanilla with baking spices and apricots.
Taste: Rye grass, apricots, vanilla, and cinnamon.
Finish: Long and spicy. Lots of cinnamon.

Susan

Nose: Caramel and rice spice with some dark fruit.
Taste: Very spicy with caramel, vanilla, and rye grass.
Finish: Long, drying to caraway and pepper.

Notes

Sugarland Distilling Company, Gatlinburg, Tennessee. Water releases a bit more fruit and reveals a cedar note.

My Score		
Notes: _____		
_____		
_____		
Appearance (1-5) ____	Nose (1-25) ____	
Taste (1-25) ____	Finish (1-25) ____	
Complexity (1-10) ____	Overall Impression (1-10) ____	
SCORE ____		

Rock Town Arkansas Rye

Proof:	92
Age:	Under 4 years
Type:	Not straight
Style:	Rye
Mash Bill:	52% rye, 38% corn, 10% malted barley
Color:	Dark Straw
Price:	$$$$

Mike

Nose: Young whiskey. Rye grass, vanilla, and a hint of oak.

Taste: Rye grass, vanilla, a little apple, and oak.

Finish: Medium long with oak and baking spices.

Susan

Nose: Rye toast, some vanilla, and faint apples.

Taste: Smoky, with rye spice, and caramel.

Finish: Pepper and oak with a little nuttiness.

Notes

Rick Town Distillery, Little Rock, Arkansas.

My Score

Notes: _____

_____

_____

Appearance (1-5) _____   Nose (1-25) _____

Taste (1-25) _____   Finish (1-25) _____

Complexity (1-10) _____   Overall Impression (1-10) _____

SCORE _____

Russell's Reserve Single Barrel Rye

Proof: 104
Age: NAS
Type: Single Barrel, Non-Chill Filtered
Style: Rye
Mash Bill: Not released
Color: Straw
Price: $$$$$

Mike

Nose: Rye grass, vanilla, peaches and apricots, with a hint of tobacco and oak.

Taste: Rye grass, vanilla, peaches, a little baking spice, and tobacco.

Finish: Long and dry with oak and a little cinnamon.

Susan

Nose: Oaky with rye spices and fruit.

Taste: Rye crackers, honey, some caramel, and baking spice.

Finish: Becomes dry very quickly, but not at all bitter.

Notes

Wild Turkey Distillery, Lawrenceburg, Kentucky. Great base for a Manhattan, but, of course, fine sipping on it's own.

My Score

Notes: _____

_____

_____

Appearance (1-5) _____   Nose (1-25) _____

Taste (1-25) _____   Finish (1-25) _____

Complexity (1-10) _____   Overall Impression (1-10) _____

SCORE _____

Sagamore Spirit Cask Stength Rye

Proof:	124
Age:	Over 3 years
Type:	Barrel Strength
Style:	Rye
Mash Bill:	High rye and low rye whiskies
Color:	Pale Straw
Price:	$$$$$

Mike

Nose:	Rye grass, vanilla, and anise. Water opens it with some caramel.
Taste:	Rye grass, licorice, and vanilla with some pepper spice. Again, water brings out caramel.
Finish:	Long and dry with oak and spice. Water weakens the finish.

Susan

Nose:	Rye grass and peppery spice.
Taste:	Fennel, anise, very herbal. Water sweetens it, revealing some fruit.
Finish:	Very quick.

Notes

Sagamore Spirit, Baltimore, Maryland. Mingling of two ryes sourced from MGP, Lawrenceburg, Indiana. Batch 2A, bottle 1423. Try this with an ice cube.

My Score

Notes: _____

_____

_____

Appearance (1-5)	____	Nose (1-25)	____
Taste (1-25)	____	Finish (1-25)	____
Complexity (1-10)	____	Overall Impression (1-10)	____

SCORE ____

Sagamore Spirit Straight Rye

Proof:	83
Age:	Over 3 years
Type:	Straight
Style:	Rye
Mash Bill:	High rye and low rye whiskies
Color:	Pale Straw
Price:	$$$$

Mike
Nose: Very light. Rye grass and vanilla. Not much else.
Taste: Rye grass, vanilla and a hint of white pepper.
Finish: Short and dry with some oak and pepper.

Susan
Nose: Rye grass, some refined sugar. Not much else.
Taste: Ripe apples, rye cereal, light vanilla and pepper.
Finish: Very dry with fading pepper.

Notes
Sagamore Spirit, Baltimore, Maryland. Mingling of two ryes sourced from MGP, Lawrenceburg, Indiana.

My Score
Notes: _____
_____
_____

Appearance (1-5) _____   Nose (1-25) _____
Taste (1-25) _____   Finish (1-25) _____
Complexity (1-10) _____   Overall Impression (1-10) _____
SCORE _____

Sazerac 18-Year Rye

Proof:	90
Age:	18 years
Type:	Straight, Extra Aged
Style:	Rye
Mash Bill:	Not released
Color:	Dark Straw
Price:	$$$$$

Mike

Nose:	Rye grass, ripe apples, old leather, and oak.
Taste:	Musty, with rye grass, ripe apples, and baking spice.
Finish:	Long and musty.

Susan

Nose:	Caramel, toffee, rye spice, dates, and leather.
Taste:	There's some corn husk that seems to dominate the other flavors such as toffee, fruit, and spices.
Finish:	Short and dry.

Notes

Buffalo Trace Distillery, Frankfort, Kentucky. One of the bottlings in the annual Antiques Collection release. This was from 2017. After letting it sit in the glass, the mustiness diminished considerably.

My Score

Notes: _____

_____

_____

Appearance (1-5)	____	Nose (1-25)	____
Taste (1-25)	____	Finish (1-25)	____
Complexity (1-10)	____	Overall Impression (1-10)	____

SCORE ____

Sazerac Rye

Proof:	90
Age:	NAS
Type:	Straight
Style:	Rye
Mash Bill:	Not released
Color:	Pale Straw
Price:	$$$

Mike
Nose: Rye grass, peaches, vanilla, and a little baking spice.

Taste: Rye grass, peaches, vanilla, and cinnamon with a little oak towards the finish.

Finish: Long and dry with cinnamon and oak.

Susan
Nose: Spicy rye grass, figs, dusting of cinnamon.

Taste: Rich mouthfeel with rye toast, dark fruit, and pepper.

Finish: Light, long, and oaky.

Notes
Buffalo Trace Distillery, Frankfort, Kentucky. Naturally, this is perfect in a Sazerac cocktail.

My Score

Notes: _____

_____

_____

Appearance (1-5)	____	Nose (1-25)	____
Taste (1-25)	____	Finish (1-25)	____
Complexity (1-10)	____	Overall Impression (1-10)	____

SCORE ____

Single Track Rye

Proof:	112
Age:	47 months
Type:	Barrel Strength
Style:	Rye
Mash Bill:	95% rye, 5% malted barley
Color:	Straw
Price:	$$$$$

Mike

Nose:	Rye grass, vanilla and a hint of anise or licorice.
Taste:	Rye grass, caramel and anise with a hint of pepper.
Finish:	Long, dry with oak and black pepper.

Susan

Nose:	Rye grass, a little vanilla, and some anise.
Taste:	Spicy rye with some peppermint and tart cherries.
Finish:	Peppery, fairly long, ends in peppermint.

Notes

Single Track Spirits, Cody, Wyoming. Surprisingly smooth at this high proof. Water reveals more spice.

My Score

Notes: _____

_____

_____

Appearance (1-5)	____	Nose (1-25)	____
Taste (1-25)	____	Finish (1-25)	____
Complexity (1-10)	____	Overall Impression (1-10)	____

SCORE ____

Sonoma County Black Truffle Rye

Proof: 100
Age: NAS
Type: Pot Distilled, Infused
Style: Rye
Mash Bill: Not released
Color: Pale Straw
Price: $$$$$ (375 mL)

Mike

Nose: Very earthy. Rye grass, mushrooms and a hint of leather.

Taste: Very earthy. Rye grass and truffles (?) with a hint of cherries and leather.

Finish: Spices come out on the finish – cinnamon, ginger and a hint of oak.

Susan

Nose: Truffle earthiness, horehound candy, and rye grass.

Taste: Caramel with ripe cherries, pepper, and truffle umami.

Finish: Long, spicy, and dry.

Notes

Sonoma County Distilling Co., Rohnert Park, California. Uses alembic pot stills. The infusion is with French Black Perigold truffles.

My Score

Notes: _____

_____

_____

Appearance (1-5) ____   Nose (1-25) ____

Taste (1-25) ____   Finish (1-25) ____

Complexity (1-10) ____   Overall Impression (1-10) ____

SCORE ____

Sonoma County Cherrywood Rye

Proof:	95.6
Age:	1 year
Type:	Pot Distilled
Style:	Rye
Mash Bill:	Canadian rye, Canadian wheat, cherry wood smoked malted barley
Color:	Pale Straw
Price:	$$$$ (375 mL)

Mike

Nose: Smoky rye grass with dates, dried cherries, and old leather.

Taste: Dried cherries and dates with smoke and leather. Cinnamon and allspice are in the background.

Finish: Long and dry with smoke and oak, but the fruit lingers.

Susan

Nose: Rye grass with some vanilla and spice.

Taste: Rye bread, apples, vanilla, and nutmeg.

Finish: Dries nicely to oak and pepper.

Notes

Sonoma County Distilling Co., Rohnert Park, California. Uses alembic pot stills. Sourced and then aged in charred American oak. Batch 2, bottle 885.

My Score

Notes: _____

_____

_____

Appearance (1-5) _____   Nose (1-25) _____

Taste (1-25) _____   Finish (1-25) _____

Complexity (1-10) _____   Overall Impression (1-10) _____

SCORE _____

Starlight Indiana Straight Single Barrel Rye 3-Year

Proof:	117.6
Age:	3 years
Type:	Single Barrel, Barrel Proof, Pot Distilled
Style:	Rye
Mash Bill:	85% rye, 15% malted barley
Color:	Straw
Price:	$$$$

Mike

Nose: Rye grass, vanilla, caramel, with some dates and berries. Just a hint of spice and oak.

Taste: Caramel, dates, allspice, and oak.

Finish: Dry with oak, spice, and a hint of fruit.

Susan

Nose: Spicy, herbal rye with some vanilla and a floral note.

Taste: Roses, figs, and pepper with a lot of oak.

Finish: Dries to peppery tannins.

Notes

Starlight Distillery, Starlight, Indiana. Barrel 1369. Water releases horehound candy and come honey.

My Score

Notes: _____

_____

_____

Appearance (1-5)	____	Nose (1-25)	____
Taste (1-25)	____	Finish (1-25)	____
Complexity (1-10)	____	Overall Impression (1-10)	____

SCORE ____

Starlight Indiana Straight Single Barrel Rye 4-Year

Proof:	114.8
Age:	4 years
Type:	Single Barrel, Barrel Proof, Pot Distilled
Style:	Rye
Mash Bill:	No corn
Color:	Dark Straw
Price:	$$$$

Mike

Nose:	Rye grass and cherries, with vanilla, spice, and oak.
Taste:	Rye grass, cherries, caramel, and nutmeg with a hint of oak.
Finish:	Long and dry with oak, nutmeg, and a little lingering cherry note.

Susan

Nose:	Brown sugar, caramel, faintest of rye spice.
Taste:	Rye asserts itself on the palate with caraway, dates, dark cherries, and marshmallows.
Finish:	Dry and peppery, but quite smooth for the high proof.

Notes

Starlight Distillery, Starlight, Indiana. Water brings out more dates and caramel.

My Score

Notes: _____

_____

_____

Appearance (1-5) ____	Nose (1-25)	____
Taste (1-25) ____	Finish (1-25)	____
Complexity (1-10) ____	Overall Impression (1-10)	____
	SCORE ____	

Still and Oak Straight Rye

Proof:	90
Age:	NAS
Type:	Straight, Non-Chill Filtered
Style:	Rye
Mash Bill:	78% rye, 22% malted barley
Color:	Light Straw
Price:	$$$

Mike

Nose:	Rye grass, Ripe pears, and vanilla with a hint of oak.
Taste:	Rye grass, vanilla, pears, and baking spices.
Finish:	Long and dry with oak and spice.

Susan

Nose:	Caramel, caraway, and oak.
Taste:	Caramel, spice, and a touch of oak.
Finish:	Long and peppery with dry tannins.

Notes

Great Lakes Distilling, Milwaukee, Wisconsin. Not an especially assertive rye, but still a very pleasant sip.

My Score

Notes: _____

_____

_____

Appearance (1-5)	____	Nose (1-25)	____
Taste (1-25)	____	Finish (1-25)	____
Complexity (1-10)	____	Overall Impression (1-10)	____

SCORE ____

Stonehouse Distillery Rye Whiskey

Proof:	90
Age:	NAS
Type:	Pot Distilled
Style:	Rye
Mash Bill:	100% rye
Color:	Barely tinted
Price:	$$$$

Mike

Nose: Rye grass and strong caramel (caramel coloring?), and witch hazel.

Taste: Rye grass and a cloying sweet flavor reminiscent of scented soap.

Finish: Short (thank god) and astringent.

Susan

Nose: Caramel, spice, and witch hazel.

Taste: Strange dishwashing liquid aroma/flavor.

Finish: Short and dry with soap suds.

Notes

Stonehouse Distillery, Winston, Montana. We hope this was an anomalous batch.

My Score

Notes: _____

_____

_____

Appearance (1-5) _____ Nose (1-25) _____

Taste (1-25) _____ Finish (1-25) _____

Complexity (1-10) _____ Overall Impression (1-10) _____

SCORE _____

Templeton Rye

Proof:	80
Age:	4 years
Type:	Not straight
Style:	Rye
Mash Bill:	95% rye, 5% malted barley
Color:	Light Straw
Price:	$$$

Mike

Nose: Very light. Vanilla and a hint of fruit and oak.

Taste: Vanilla with some juicy fruit gum. There's also some baking spice and oak.

Finish: Medium long with oak, spice, and lingering fruit.

Susan

Nose: Very faint with whispers of apple, mint, and baking spices.

Taste: Vanilla cream filling in wafer cookies. Some sweet cherries.

Finish: Very quickly dries to oak.

Notes

Templeton Rye Spirits LLC, Templeton, Iowa. Sourced from MGP in Lawrenceburg, Indiana.

My Score

Notes: _____

_____

_____

Appearance (1-5)	____	Nose (1-25)	____
Taste (1-25)	____	Finish (1-25)	____
Complexity (1-10)	____	Overall Impression (1-10)	____

SCORE ____

Thirteenth Colony Southern Rye Whiskey

Proof:	95
Age:	NAS
Type:	Finished
Style:	Rye
Mash Bill:	96% rye, 4% malted barley
Color:	Pale Straw
Price:	$$$

Mike

Nose:	Rye grass, peaches, and vanilla with a hint of spice.
Taste:	Rye grass, peaches, and baking spice.
Finish:	Medium long with oak and spice.

Susan

Nose:	Rye grass, vanilla, new leather, some horehound.
Taste:	Vanilla, nutmeg, rye spice, but not complex overall.
Finish:	Starts sweet and dries to oak.

Notes

Produced and bottled by Thirteenth Colony Distilleries LLC, Americus, Georgia. Finished by adding French oak spirals to the barrel.

My Score

Notes: _____

_____

_____

Appearance (1-5) ____	Nose (1-25)	____
Taste (1-25) ____	Finish (1-25)	____
Complexity (1-10) ____	Overall Impression (1-10)	____
	SCORE ____	

Tom's Foolery Rye

Proof:	90
Age:	3 years, 3 month
Type:	Pot Distilled, Single Barrel
Style:	Rye
Mash Bill:	100% rye including malted rye
Color:	Dark Straw
Price:	$$$$

Mike

Nose: Rye grass, some honeysuckle floral notes, and oak.

Taste: Rye grass, apples, a bit of vanilla and honey with oak and pepper spice.

Finish: Long and dry with oak and pepper.

Susan

Nose: Rye grass, some caramel, rye spice, and sweet floral note.

Taste: Rye herbs, vanilla, caramel, and some apples and cinnamon.

Finish: Long and spicy.

Notes

Tom's Foolery Distillery, Burton, Ohio. Farm to glass distillery uses a pot still for all products. This would make a splendid Manhattan with the best vermouth. Treat it with respect. Barrel 237, bottle 34.

My Score

Notes: _____

_____

_____

Appearance (1-5) ____	Nose (1-25)	____
Taste (1-25) ____	Finish (1-25)	____
Complexity (1-10) ____	Overall Impression (1-10)	____

SCORE ____

Town Branch Rye Whiskey

Proof:	100
Age:	NAS
Type:	Pot Distilled
Style:	Rye
Mash Bill:	55% rye, 30% corn, 15% malted barley
Color:	Dark Straw
Price:	$$$$

Mike

Nose: Very fruity. Apples and pears with some honeysuckle floral notes.

Taste: Rye grass and apples with a hint of pepper and cinnamon.

Finish: Long and peppery with just a hint of oak.

Susan

Nose: Strongly herbal rye with some spiced peaches.

Taste: Very smooth for 100 proof. Rye and spice notes predominate, but it is also faintly medicinal.

Finish: Surprisingly sweet at first before drying to oak.

Notes

Alltech's Lexington Distilling Co., Lexington, Kentucky. Distilled in duel copper pot stills.

My Score

Notes: _____

_____

_____

Appearance (1-5)	____	Nose (1-25)	____
Taste (1-25)	____	Finish (1-25)	____
Complexity (1-10)	____	Overall Impression (1-10)	____

SCORE ____

WhistlePig Farmstock Rye

Proof: 86
Age: 2 years
Type: Not straight
Style: Rye
Mash Bill: 100% rye (see notes)
Color: Very Pale Straw
Price: $$$$$

Mike

Nose: Very light nose of vanilla and rye grass.
Taste: Vanilla, rye grass, and a bit of earthy grain musk.
Finish: Short, with a bit of pepper and oak.

Susan

Nose: Rye grass, cellulose, a little caraway.
Taste: Rye grass, cinnamon, vanilla, caramel.
Finish: Long and herbal.

Notes

WhistlePig, Shoreham, Vermont. Sourced product – 32% 2-year Vermont whiskey made on site, 45% from MGP, Lawrenceburg, Indiana, 23% a 10-year Canadian rye. Label states it is "Bottled in Barn."

My Score

Notes: _____

_____

Appearance (1-5) ____   Nose (1-25) ____
Taste (1-25) ____   Finish (1-25) ____
Complexity (1-10) ____   Overall Impression (1-10) ____
SCORE ____

WhistlePig Straight Rye

Proof:	100
Age:	10 years
Type:	Finished, Extra Aged
Style:	Rye
Mash Bill:	100% rye
Color:	Pale Straw
Price:	$$$$$

Mike

Nose: Rye grass, vanilla, and some baking spice.

Taste: Rye grass, vanilla, and cinnamon with a little oak.

Finish: Long and dry with earthy oak.

Susan

Nose: Rye grass, a little caramel, and baking spices.

Taste: Rye grass, sweet mint, some ripe apple/pear.

Finish: Dry with black pepper.

Notes

WhistlePig, Shoreham, Vermont. Sourced whiskey from Canada. Finished in ex-bourbon barrels.

My Score

Notes: _____

_____

_____

Appearance (1-5)	____	Nose (1-25)	____
Taste (1-25)	____	Finish (1-25)	____
Complexity (1-10)	____	Overall Impression (1-10)	____

SCORE ____

WhistlePig The Boss Hog

Proof:	116.6
Age:	14 years
Type:	Finished, Extra Aged
Style:	Rye
Mash Bill:	100% rye
Color:	Straw
Price:	$$$$$$

Mike

Nose: Caramel, prunes and dates, with hints of rye grass and oak.

Taste: Caramel, dates and berries, baking spice, and oak.

Finish: Long and dry with oak and spice.

Susan

Nose: Rye toast, dark fruit, and vanilla.

Taste: Rye toast with jam and spice.

Finish: Very warm and stays sweet until pepper pops at the very end.

Notes

WhistlePig, Shoreham, Vermont. Sourced whiskey from Canada. Finished in ex-Armagnac barrels. Barrel 23, Fourth Edition – The Black Prince.

My Score

Notes: _____

_____

_____

Appearance (1-5) ____ Nose (1-25) ____

Taste (1-25) ____ Finish (1-25) ____

Complexity (1-10) ____ Overall Impression (1-10) ____

SCORE ____

Widow Jane Oak

Proof:	91
Age:	NAS
Type:	Finished
Style:	Rye
Mash Bill:	Not released
Color:	Very, Very Pale Straw
Price:	$$$$

Mike

Nose: Pineapples, vanilla, and rye grass.

Taste: Pineapples, vanilla, rye grass, and oak.

Finish: Short and sweet with fruit and vanilla.

Susan

Nose: Rye grass, cinnamon, ripe fruit.

Taste: Tropical fruit (mango?) with spicy tannins.

Finish: Long and peppery, leaving tingling lips.

Notes

Widow Jane Distillery, Brooklyn, New York. Finished with oak staves. Very different, interesting whiskey.

My Score

Notes: _____

_____

_____

Appearance (1-5)	____	Nose (1-25)	____
Taste (1-25)	____	Finish (1-25)	____
Complexity (1-10)	____	Overall Impression (1-10)	____

SCORE ____

Widow Jane Oak and Applewood Rye

Proof: 91
Age: NAS
Type: Finished
Style: Rye
Mash Bill: Not released
Color: Almost Clear
Price: $$$$

Mike

Nose: Rye grass, Juicy Fruit gum, vanilla, and a hint of spice.

Taste: Very sweet and fruity. The gum with a little baking spice and oak.

Finish: Medium long and dry with oak.

Susan

Nose: Lot sand lots of rye grass with some cellulose and sweet, scented candles.

Taste: Sweet grains, apples, and cinnamon.

Finish: Medium, drying to spicy oak.

Notes

Widow Jane Distillery, Brooklyn, New York. Seven-year-old rye finished with oak and applewood staves, Kosher.

My Score

Notes: _____

_____

_____

Appearance (1-5) ____   Nose (1-25) ____

Taste (1-25) ____   Finish (1-25) ____

Complexity (1-10) ____   Overall Impression (1-10) ____

SCORE ____

Wild Turkey Rye

Proof:	81
Age:	NAS
Type:	Straight
Style:	Rye
Mash Bill:	Not released
Color:	Very Pale Straw
Price:	$$

Mike

Nose:	Rye grass, honey, and leather with a hint of oak.
Taste:	Rye grass, vanilla, with a hint of cherries or berries and baking spices, including ginger.
Finish:	Short, but dry with oak and spice.

Susan

Nose:	Quite light, with a whiff of rye and some brown sugar and spice.
Taste:	Rye grass, some vanilla, and pepper.
Finish:	Starts sweet and dries to a gingery ending.

Notes

Wild Turkey Distillery, Lawrenceburg, Kentucky. Reliable, bargain priced rye for cocktails.

My Score

Notes: _____

_____

_____

Appearance (1-5)	____	Nose (1-25)	____
Taste (1-25)	____	Finish (1-25)	____
Complexity (1-10)	____	Overall Impression (1-10)	____

SCORE ____

Wilderness Trail Settler's Select Rye

Proof:	97
Age:	NAS
Type:	Single Barrel, Non-Chill Filtered
Style:	Rye
Mash Bill:	56% rye, 33% corn, 11% malted barley
Color:	Pale Straw
Price:	$$$$$

Mike

Nose: Rye grass, citrus, and vanilla with a hint of oak.

Taste: Rye grass, vanilla, pepper spice, and orange zest.

Finish: Long, dry, and spicy.

Susan

Nose: Caramel, a little pepper spice, and coconut.

Taste: Rye crisp, some caramel apple, and oak.

Finish: Long and spicy.

Notes

Wilderness Trail Distillery, Danville, Kentucky. Barrel 15D22, bottle 84/210. Sweet mash process.

My Score

Notes: _____

_____

_____

Appearance (1-5) _____   Nose (1-25) _____

Taste (1-25) _____   Finish (1-25) _____

Complexity (1-10) _____   Overall Impression (1-10) _____

SCORE _____

Willett Family Estate Small Batch Rye

Proof: 112.2
Age: 3 years
Type: Straight, Small Batch
Style: Rye
Mash Bill: Not released
Color: Dark Straw
Price: $$$$$$

Mike

Nose: Pears and berries with vanilla, rye grass, and a hint of baking spices.

Taste: Very fruity with berries and dates. Also, nutmeg and cinnamon with vanilla and oak in the background.

Finish: Long and dry with oak and spice.

Susan

Nose: Spicy rye with eucalyptus and some dried cherries.

Taste: Freshly baked dark rye bread with cherries, cinnamon, and eucalyptus.

Finish: Long and dry.

Notes

Willett Distillery, Bardstown, Kentucky. For Mike, water enhances the oak and increased the burn. For Susan, water amplified the cherries and eucalyptus. A very different sip.

My Score

Notes: _____

_____

_____

Appearance (1-5) _____   Nose (1-25) _____

Taste (1-25) _____   Finish (1-25) _____

Complexity (1-10) _____   Overall Impression (1-10) _____

SCORE _____

Woodford Reserve Kentucky Straight Rye Whiskey

Proof:	90.4
Age:	NAS
Type:	Straight, Small Batch
Style:	Rye
Mash Bill:	53% rye
Color:	Straw
Price:	$$$$

Mike
Nose: Rye gras, vanilla, and a hint of fruit.
Taste: Rye grass, vanilla, pepper spice, and apples.
Finish: Long, dry, and spicy.

Susan
Nose: Rye grass, peaches, and a little sweet oak.
Taste: Vanilla and hazelnuts, with some orchard fruit and light oak.
Finish: Dries to a light oak note.

Notes
Woodford Reserve Distillery, Versailles, Kentucky. Batch 89, bottle 561.

My Score

Notes: _____

_____

_____

Appearance (1-5) _____   Nose (1-25) _____

Taste (1-25) _____   Finish (1-25) _____

Complexity (1-10) _____   Overall Impression (1-10) _____

SCORE _____

Woodinville Rye

Proof:	90
Age:	NAS
Type:	Pot Distilled
Style:	Rye
Mash Bill:	100% rye
Color:	Pale Amber
Price:	$$$$

Mike

Nose: Rye grass, caramel, hint of sweet spices, and oak.

Taste: Rye grass, caramel, pears, and baking spice with a hint of oak.

Finish: Long. Dry oak and spice with a hint of tobacco.

Susan

Nose: Burnt toffee, rye spice, and some dark fruit.

Taste: Predominantly caramel with a little cinnamon and some dark fruit such as dates.

Finish: Very dry.

Notes

Woodinville Distillery, Woodinville, Washington. Very sippable, but not complex.

My Score

Notes: _____

_____

_____

Appearance (1-5)	____	Nose (1-25)	____
Taste (1-25)	____	Finish (1-25)	____
Complexity (1-10)	____	Overall Impression (1-10)	____

SCORE ____

Yippee Ki-Yay

Proof:	92
Age:	NAS
Type:	Finished
Style:	Rye
Mash Bill:	Not disclosed
Color:	Dark Straw
Price:	$$$$$

Mike

Nose: Very fruity, with berries and cherries, vanilla, and a hint of oak.

Taste: Fruity with raspberry and cherries. Plus, vanilla, baking spice, oak and rye grass.

Finish: Dry with oak and some raspberry.

Susan

Nose: Rye herbs, lots of spice, some caramel and raspberries.

Taste: Lots of vanilla accompanies toasted rye roll and carraway with some baking spice.

Finish: Long and spicy.

Notes

High West Distillery, Park City, Utah. Blend of straight ryes, 2-16 years old, finished in vermouth and shiraz barrels. Wine finishing lends sweetness, but does not overpower.

My Score

Notes: _____

_____

_____

Appearance (1-5) _____   Nose (1-25) _____

Taste (1-25) _____   Finish (1-25) _____

Complexity (1-10) _____   Overall Impression (1-10) _____

SCORE _____

Additional Rye Whiskey Releases

Name: _____

Distillery: _____

Proof: _____ **Mash Bill:** _____
Age: _____ _____
Type: _____ **Color:** _____
Style: _____ **Price:** _____

My Score

Notes: _____
_____
_____

Appearance (1-5) _____ Nose (1-25) _____
Taste (1-25) _____ Finish (1-25) _____
Complexity (1-10) _____ Overall Impression (1-10) _____
SCORE _____

Name: _____

Distillery: _____

Proof: _____ **Mash Bill:** _____
Age: _____ _____
Type: _____ **Color:** _____
Style: _____ **Price:** _____

My Score

Notes: _____
_____
_____

Appearance (1-5) _____ Nose (1-25) _____
Taste (1-25) _____ Finish (1-25) _____
Complexity (1-10) _____ Overall Impression (1-10) _____
SCORE _____

Chapter Eight
Tennessee Whiskey

Tennessee whiskey is different from Bourbon whiskey in that they distillers filter the new make spirit through sugar maple charcoal before entering the whiskey into the oak container. In all other ways it is a Bourbon Whiskey. It is recognized as a Bourbon by the export markets. However, the Jack Daniel and George Dickel distilleries spent decades proclaiming themselves as a unique style of whiskey and rightly so. It does have an additional smoky characteristic that is not found in Bourbon. In the 21st century there have been many artisan distilleries built in Tennessee that are now producing Tennessee whiskey of their own.

Gentleman Jack

Proof:	80
Age:	NAS
Type:	Not straight
Style:	Tennessee
Mash Bill:	80% corn, 8% rye, 12% malted barley
Color:	Pale Straw
Price:	$$$

Mike
Nose: Bananas Foster – vanilla and banana with a bit of smoke.

Taste: Banana and corn with vanilla and smoke.

Finish: Very light, but smoky.

Susan
Nose: Banana, cornbread.

Taste: Very sweet. Candy corn and cinnamon-sprinkled banana.

Finish: Short and dry.

Notes
Jack Daniel Distillery, Lynchburg, Tennessee. Filtered a second time after aging and before bottling. Owned by Louisville-based Brown-Forman Corp.

My Score

Notes: _____

_____

_____

Appearance (1-5)	____	Nose (1-25)	____
Taste (1-25)	____	Finish (1-25)	____
Complexity (1-10)	____	Overall Impression (1-10)	____

SCORE ____

George Dickel Barrel Select

Proof:	86
Age:	NAS
Type:	Small Batch
Style:	Tennessee
Mash Bill:	84% corn, 8% rye, 8% malted barley
Color:	Straw
Price:	$$$$$

Mike

Nose: Ripe apples, caramel, maple smoke and baking spices.

Taste: Caramel apples, baking spice and maple smoke with a hint of oak.

Finish: Dry with spices and oak and a hint of smoke.

Susan

Nose: Caramel, toffee, dark fruit.

Taste: Toasted pecans, more toffee, new leather and a sprinkling of cocoa.

Finish: Rather light, but smooth and dry.

Notes

George A. Dickel & Company, Tullahoma, Tennessee. A very elegant sipping whiskey.

My Score

Notes: _____

_____

_____

Appearance (1-5) ____   Nose (1-25) ____

Taste (1-25) ____   Finish (1-25) ____

Complexity (1-10) ____   Overall Impression (1-10) ____

SCORE ____

George Dickel
Bottled-in-Bond

Proof:	100
Age:	13 years
Type:	Bonded, Extra Aged
Style:	Tennessee
Mash Bill:	84% corn, 8% rye, 8% malted barley
Color:	Pale Straw
Price:	$$$$

Mike

Nose: Flintstones cherry vitamin mineral note, smoke, oak, and caramel.

Taste: Vanilla, creamed corn, smoke, apples, pepper spice and leather. Very complex.

Finish: Long and dry with smoke, oak, and pepper.

Susan

Nose: Roasted corn, sugar-coated cherries.

Taste: Surprisingly spicy. Then fruity chewable vitamins appear followed by corn and oak.

Finish: Dries quickly to oak.

Notes

George Dickel Cascade Hollow Distillery, Tullahoma, Tennessee. Very different. You will probably either love it or hate it.

My Score

Notes: _____

_____

_____

Appearance (1-5) _____   Nose (1-25) _____

Taste (1-25) _____   Finish (1-25) _____

Complexity (1-10) _____   Overall Impression (1-10) _____

SCORE _____

George Dickel Cascade Hollow

Proof:	80
Age:	3 years
Type:	Not straight
Style:	Tennessee
Mash Bill:	84% corn, 8% rye, 8% malted barley
Color:	Very Pale Straw
Price:	$$$

Mike

Nose: Very light. Corn, smoke, and a little vanilla.

Taste: Vanilla, corn, and smoke with a hint of pepper and a hint of maple in the background.

Finish: Short and dry with pepper and oak.

Susan

Nose: Corn, stewed apples, very light spice with some vanilla.

Taste: More corn, some new leather, spearmint.

Finish: Long for the proof strength, with minty sweetness drying to oak.

Notes

George A. Dickel & Company, Tullahoma, Tennessee. Light sip. Not complex.

My Score

Notes: _____

_____

_____

Appearance (1-5)	____	Nose (1-25)	____
Taste (1-25)	____	Finish (1-25)	____
Complexity (1-10)	____	Overall Impression (1-10)	____

SCORE ____

George Dickel Distillery Reserve

Proof:	87
Age:	17 years
Type:	Extra Aged
Style:	Tennessee
Mash Bill:	84% corn, 8% rye, 8% malted barley
Color:	Pale Straw
Price:	$$$$$ (375 mL)

Mike

Nose: Caramel, smoke and a bit of leather and spice.

Taste: Rich caramel, oak, and pepper with a little ripe apple fruit.

Finish: Dry with oak, smoke, and pepper.

Susan

Nose: Apples, some peach, and vanilla.

Taste: Sweet Thai style curry and grain with a little mint.

Finish: Becomes very flat and dry with a touch of peppery oak.

Notes

George A. Dickel & Company, Tullahoma, Tennessee. Very light color for 17 years old. Low proof and filtering may have taken out the color. We would love to try this at barrel proof.

My Score

Notes: _____

_____

_____

Appearance (1-5) ____		Nose (1-25) ____
Taste (1-25) ____		Finish (1-25) ____
Complexity (1-10) ____		Overall Impression (1-10) ____

SCORE ____

George Dickel No. 8

Proof:	80
Age:	NAS
Type:	Not straight
Style:	Tennessee
Mash Bill:	84% corn, 8% rye, 8% malted barley
Color:	Pale Straw
Price:	$$

Mike
Nose: Corn and vanilla with a little smoke and apples.

Taste: Corn, vanilla, apples, and smoke with a hint of black pepper.

Finish: Long and dry with oak and pepper.

Susan
Nose: Cherries with light apricot in the background.

Taste: Caramel and sweet oak and apples. Thin mouthfeel.

Finish: Sweet and peppery with pleasant tannins.

Notes
George A. Dickel & Company, Tullahoma, Tennessee.

My Score

Notes: _____

_____

_____

Appearance (1-5)	____	Nose (1-25)	____
Taste (1-25)	____	Finish (1-25)	____
Complexity (1-10)	____	Overall Impression (1-10)	____

SCORE ____

George Dickel No. 12

Proof:	90
Age:	NAS
Type:	Not straight
Style:	Tennessee
Mash Bill:	84% corn, 8% rye, 8% malted barley
Color:	Pale Straw
Price:	$$

Mike
Nose: Vanilla and honey with a bit of smoke and apples. Some baking spices in the background.
Taste: Caramel, smoke, and apples – apple pie with nutmeg and cinnamon.
Finish: Long, dry with oak, smoke, and spices.

Susan
Nose: Vanilla, cherries, and almonds.
Taste: More vanilla and fruit with some marzipan.
Finish: Dries to oak and pepper, but not hot.

Notes
George A. Dickel & Company, Tullahoma, Tennessee. Just a few drops of water amplify the fruit and almonds.

My Score
Notes: _____

_____

_____

Appearance (1-5)	____	Nose (1-25)	____
Taste (1-25)	____	Finish (1-25)	____
Complexity (1-10)	____	Overall Impression (1-10)	____

SCORE ____

Jack Daniel's Single Barrel Select

Proof:	131.7
Age:	NAS
Type:	Barrel Proof
Style:	Tennessee
Mash Bill:	80% corn, 8% rye, 12% malted barley
Color:	Dark Straw
Price:	$$$$$

Mike

Nose: Smokey, with a hint of vanilla and bananas.
Taste: Rich caramel, bananas, pepper, and smoke.
Finish: Long and dry with oak and pepper.

Susan

Nose: Caramel, baked apples, baking spices.
Taste: Alcohol overwhelms until water is added, which brings out some fruit and nuttiness.
Finish: Hot.

Notes

Jack Daniel Distillery, Lynchburg, Tennessee. Owned by Louisville-based Brown-Forman Corp. Even after adding water, this whiskey is still hot and oaky.

My Score

Notes: _____

_____

_____

Appearance (1-5) _____   Nose (1-25) _____

Taste (1-25) _____   Finish (1-25) _____

Complexity (1-10) _____   Overall Impression (1-10) _____

SCORE _____

Jack Daniel's Old No. 7

Proof:	80
Age:	NAS
Type:	Not straight
Style:	Tennessee
Mash Bill:	80% corn, 8% rye, 12% malted barley
Color:	Pale Straw
Price:	$$

Mike

Nose:	Vanilla, corn, bananas, and smoke.
Taste:	Vanilla and smoke with some banana and pepper.
Finish:	Dry and peppery.

Susan

Nose:	Banana, corn, and some apples.
Taste:	Sugar-glazed banana and vanilla.
Finish:	Warm with a touch of astringency.

Notes

Jack Daniel Distillery, Lynchburg, Tennessee. Owned by Louisville-based Brown-Forman Corp. This is the largest selling American whiskey in the world.

My Score

Notes: _____

_____

_____

Appearance (1-5)	____	Nose (1-25)	____
Taste (1-25)	____	Finish (1-25)	____
Complexity (1-10)	____	Overall Impression (1-10)	____

SCORE ____

Uncle Nearest 1856 Premium Whiskey

Proof: 100
Age: NAS
Type: Small Batch
Style: Tennessee
Mash Bill: 84% corn, 8% rye, 8% malted barley
Color: Pale Straw
Price: $$$$$

Mike
Nose: Vanilla and fruit – bananas – with a hint of smoke and pepper.
Taste: Vanilla and corn with bananas and maple smoke. There's a hint of pepper leading into the finish.
Finish: Dry, but short with smoke, oak, and pepper.

Susan
Nose: Vanilla, faint peach, a touch of sweet spice.
Taste: Vanilla pudding with a little cinnamon and light fruit.
Finish: Lingering mouthfeel with vanilla and oak.

Notes
Uncle Nearest Premium Whiskey, Tennessee. Honors the freed slave, Nathan "Nearest" Green, who taught Jack Daniel how to distill. Originally sourced from two undisclosed Tennessee distilleries. Currently made by a distillery in Nashville. The company is building a distillery in Shelbyville, Tennessee.

My Score

Notes: _____

_____

_____

Appearance (1-5) ____   Nose (1-25) ____
Taste (1-25) ____   Finish (1-25) ____
Complexity (1-10) ____   Overall Impression (1-10) ____
SCORE ____

Additional Tennessee Whiskey Releases

Name: _____

Distillery: _____

Proof: _____   **Mash Bill:** _____

Age: _____

Type: _____   **Color:** _____

Style: _____   **Price:** _____

My Score

Notes: _____

_____

_____

Appearance (1-5) ____   Nose (1-25) ____

Taste (1-25) ____   Finish (1-25) ____

Complexity (1-10) ____   Overall Impression (1-10) ____

SCORE ____

Name: _____

Distillery: _____

Proof: _____   **Mash Bill:** _____

Age: _____

Type: _____   **Color:** _____

Style: _____   **Price:** _____

My Score

Notes: _____

_____

_____

Appearance (1-5) ____   Nose (1-25) ____

Taste (1-25) ____   Finish (1-25) ____

Complexity (1-10) ____   Overall Impression (1-10) ____

SCORE ____

Chapter Nine
Wheat Whiskey

Wheat whiskey was produced in the years before prohibition, but it died during those long, dry years of prohibition. This changed when Heaven Hill introduced Bernheim Wheat Whiskey in 2005. They brought this style of whiskey back from the dead, and many artisan distilleries have started to produce their own brands of wheat whiskey.

77 Whiskey New York Wheat

Proof:	90
Age:	320 days
Type:	Not straight
Style:	Wheat
Mash Bill:	Wheat
Color:	Pale Straw
Price:	$$$$

Mike

Nose: Vanilla and citrus with a hint of spice and oak.

Taste: Vanilla and hazelnuts with some pepper and oak.

Finish: Long and pleasant with oak and a lot of pepper.

Susan

Nose: Herbal, with some caramel and dried fruit.

Taste: Mild pepper at first. Then fruit and vanilla with some smoke.

Finish: Fruit persists on the finish.

Notes

Breuckelen Distilling, Brooklyn, New York. Nice whiskey. Would love to try this with some more age on it.

My Score

Notes: _____

_____

_____

Appearance (1-5)	____	Nose (1-25)	____
Taste (1-25)	____	Finish (1-25)	____
Complexity (1-10)	____	Overall Impression (1-10)	____
	SCORE ____		

Bare Knuckle American Wheat Whiskey

Proof:	90
Age:	1 year minimum
Type:	Not straight
Style:	Wheat
Mash Bill:	60% wheat, 30% rye, 10% malted barley
Color:	Pale Straw
Price:	$$$

Mike
Nose: Cereal grains and vanilla, very light.

Taste: Vanilla and fruit. Berries and apples with some baking spice.

Finish: Slightly dry with oak and spice.

Susan
Nose: Light nose with wheat flakes and some faint spice.

Taste: Wheat cereal with dried apple slices.

Finish: Warm, dry ending.

Notes
KO Distilling, Manassas, Virginia. Very young, but quite good.

My Score

Notes: _____

_____

_____

Appearance (1-5) _____   Nose (1-25) _____

Taste (1-25) _____   Finish (1-25) _____

Complexity (1-10) _____   Overall Impression (1-10) _____

SCORE _____

Bernheim Original Kentucky Straight Wheat Whiskey

Proof:	90
Age:	7 years
Type:	Straight
Style:	Wheat
Mash Bill:	51% wheat, 39% rye, 10% malted barley
Color:	Light Amber
Price:	$$$

Mike

Nose: Very soft nose. Caramel, vanilla and a hint of hazelnuts.

Taste: Caramel, apples and pears with a little peppery spice and oak.

Finish: Dry with oak and pepper.

Susan

Nose: Sweet corn, vanilla, peaches, and a sprinkling of nutmeg.

Taste: Buttered corn, more nutmeg and fruit with some peppery spice, too.

Finish: Long and spicy dying to oak.

Notes

Heaven Hill Distillery, Louisville, Kentucky. This is a very smooth sip with a peppery kick.

My Score

Notes: _____

_____

_____

Appearance (1-5) ____	Nose (1-25)	____
Taste (1-25) ____	Finish (1-25)	____
Complexity (1-10) ____	Overall Impression (1-10)	____
	SCORE ____	

Buggy Whip Wheat Whiskey

Proof: 90
Age: NAS
Type: Not straight
Style: Wheat
Mash Bill: 100% organic Michigan wheat
Color: Straw
Price: $$$$

Mike
Nose: Cotton candy vanilla with some berries and oak.
Taste: Rich vanilla, berries and baking spice with a little oak and pecans.
Finish: Starts sweet. Then the spice and oak kick in for a drier ending.

Susan
Nose: Little nose with a bit of wheat cracker and hints of fruit and spice.
Taste: Vanilla and some oak with a bit of fruit and nuts.
Finish: A note of peaches appears at the very end, along with sweet oak.

Notes
Journeyman Distillery, Three Oaks, Michigan. Batch 42, bottle 599.

My Score

Notes: _____

_____

_____

Appearance (1-5) _____   Nose (1-25) _____

Taste (1-25) _____   Finish (1-25) _____

Complexity (1-10) _____   Overall Impression (1-10) _____

SCORE _____

Dry Fly Straight Washington Wheat Whiskey

Proof:	90
Age:	3 years
Type:	Straight
Style:	Wheat
Mash Bill:	100% local soft white wheat
Color:	Light Straw
Price:	$$$$

Mike

Nose: Vanilla and oak. Very light. Not much there.

Taste: Vanilla and citrus with some pepper spice and oak.

Finish: Very long and dry, but there's a hint of medicinal astringency.

Susan

Nose: Very light with some vanilla wafers and faint coconut.

Taste: Sweet with some pears and a touch of honey and slivered almonds.

Finish: Very dry with some lingering nuttiness.

Notes

Dry Fly Distilling, Spokane, Washington.

My Score

Notes: _____

_____

_____

Appearance (1-5) ____	Nose (1-25) ____
Taste (1-25) ____	Finish (1-25) ____
Complexity (1-10) ____	Overall Impression (1-10) ____

SCORE ____

Dry Fly Wheat Whiskey Cask Strength

Proof:	120
Age:	3 years
Type:	Barrel Proof
Style:	Wheat
Mash Bill:	100% organic Michigan wheat
Color:	Very Pale Straw
Price:	$$$$$

Mike

Nose: Almonds and dates with a little vanilla.

Taste: Dates and vanilla with a little baking spice and oak.

Finish: Long and slightly astringent.

Susan

Nose: Lightly floral with sweet fruit and a pinch of ginger.

Taste: Crème brulee, apples, and quite a bit of pepper.

Finish: Peppery (No doubt the high proof accounts for this).

Notes

Dry Fly Distilling, Spokane, Washington. Add water to sweeten and bring out cinnamon, nutmeg, ginger, and a little mint.

My Score		
Notes: _____		
_____		
_____		
Appearance (1-5) ____	Nose (1-25)	____
Taste (1-25) ____	Finish (1-25)	____
Complexity (1-10) ____	Overall Impression (1-10)	____
SCORE ____		

Dry Fly Wheat Whiskey Port Barrel Finish

Proof:	90
Age:	3 years
Type:	Finished
Style:	Wheat
Mash Bill:	100% organic Michigan wheat
Color:	Dark Straw
Price:	$$$$

Mike

Nose: Almonds and grapes with a little vanilla oak.

Taste: Grapes, vanilla, some cinnamon spice and oak.

Finish: Long and spicy after a fruity start.

Susan

Nose: Sweet cherries with some vanilla and faint baking spice.

Taste: Notes with fruity notes from the port barrel and plenty of cinnamon spice.

Finish: Very peppery.

Notes

Dry Fly Distilling, Spokane, Washington. After aging, whiskey is put into port barrels for 6 to 12 months.

My Score	
Notes: _____	
_____	
_____	
Appearance (1-5) ____	Nose (1-25) ____
Taste (1-25) ____	Finish (1-25) ____
Complexity (1-10) ____	Overall Impression (1-10) ____
SCORE ____	

Fearless Wheat Whiskey

Proof:	85
Age:	NAS
Type:	Straight
Style:	Wheat
Mash Bill:	At least 51% red winter wheat
Color:	Light Amber
Price:	$$$$

Mike

Nose: Very light. Vanilla and pecans with a hint of pears.

Taste: Vanilla, pears, pecans with a hint of oak.

Finish: Short and dry with sweet oak.

Susan

Nose: Vanilla and custard apple with some baking spices.

Taste: Crème brulee, baked apples, and cinnamon.

Finish: Nicely warm, drying to peppery oak.

Notes

Catskill Distilling Company, Bethel, New York. Matured in 25-gallon charred oak casks.

My Score

Notes: _____

_____

_____

Appearance (1-5) _____   Nose (1-25) _____

Taste (1-25) _____   Finish (1-25) _____

Complexity (1-10) _____   Overall Impression (1-10) _____

SCORE _____

Lion's Pride Dark Wheat Whiskey

Proof: 80
Age: NAS
Type: Single Barrel, Organic
Style: Wheat
Mash Bill: Wheat
Color: Very Pale Straw
Price: $$$$

Mike
Nose: Plums, vanilla, and old leather.
Taste: Plums, vanilla, pepper spice, and oak.
Finish: Long with black pepper.

Susan
Nose: Light resin, like violin bow rosin. Some vanilla and leather.
Taste: Mostly vanilla with a fair amount of pepper.
Finish: Sort and spicy.

Notes
Koval Distillery, Chicago, Illinois. Barrel 79.

My Score		
Notes: _____		
_____		
_____		
Appearance (1-5) ____	Nose (1-25)	____
Taste (1-25) ____	Finish (1-25)	____
Complexity (1-10) ____	Overall Impression (1-10)	____
SCORE ____		

Parker's Heritage Kentucky Straight Wheat Whiskey

Proof: 127.4
Age: 13 years
Type: Barrel Proof
Style: Wheat
Mash Bill: At least 51% wheat
Color: Light Amber
Price: $$$$$

Mike

Nose: Caramel, hazelnuts and hints of apples and apricots. Water adds a little old leather.

Taste: Caramel apples and nuts with some pepper spice. Water softens the pepper.

Finish: Long and spicy with pepper and oak. Water adds a little sweetness.

Susan

Nose: Light vanilla, sweet apples, almonds verging on marzipan.

Taste: Apples, almonds, and vanilla. Matches the nose.

Finish: Lingering sweetness. Not surprisingly, water adds fruit and baking spices.

Notes

Heaven Hill Distillery, Louisville, Kentucky. Limited release. Try this one in a well-stocked whiskey bar. Bottles on the secondary market can fetch triple the original retail price of $90, and more.

My Score

Notes: _____

_____

_____

Appearance (1-5) ____   Nose (1-25) ____

Taste (1-25) ____   Finish (1-25) ____

Complexity (1-10) ____   Overall Impression (1-10) ____

SCORE ____

Pitchfork Michigan Wheat

Proof:	90
Age:	14 months
Type:	Not straight
Style:	Wheat
Mash Bill:	Malted wheat and barley
Color:	Straw
Price:	$$$$

Mike
Nose: Apricots and vanilla with a hint of pears.

Taste: Apricots, vanilla, pepper spice, oak, and a hint of chocolate.

Finish: Long and dry with oak and pepper.

Susan
Nose: Hard candy, vanilla fudge, and a tiny whiff of cinnamon.

Taste: Sweet fruit with some honey quickly changes to pepper and oak.

Finish: Quite dry and spicy.

Notes
New Holland Artisan Spirits, Holland and Grand Rapids, Michigan. Like Rogue, they are also a craft brewery. May as well distill some of that beer!

My Score

Notes: _____

_____

_____

Appearance (1-5) _____   Nose (1-25) _____

Taste (1-25) _____   Finish (1-25) _____

Complexity (1-10) _____   Overall Impression (1-10) _____

SCORE _____

Single Track Spirits Wheat Whiskey

Proof:	119
Age:	66 months
Type:	Barrel Proof
Style:	Wheat
Mash Bill:	93% Wyoming wheat, 7% malted barley
Color:	Light amber
Price:	$$$$$

Mike

Nose: Very light apricots and vanilla and a hint of oak.

Taste: Black liquorice with caramel and oak.

Finish: Long and lingering black liquorice.

Susan

Nose: Caramel, dates, brown sugar.

Taste: Sweet anise with cardamom and cloves. Imagine a South Asian fruit cake.

Finish: Warm and peppery.

Notes

Single Track Spirits, Cody, Wyoming. Made in a 250 gallon pot still. Very approachable and smooth for cask strength. Water sweetens it.

My Score

Notes: _____

_____

_____

Appearance (1-5)	____	Nose (1-25)	____
Taste (1-25)	____	Finish (1-25)	____
Complexity (1-10)	____	Overall Impression (1-10)	____

SCORE ____

TOPO Eight Oak Carolina Whiskey

Proof:	92
Age:	NAS
Type:	Finished, Organic
Style:	Wheat
Mash Bill:	Wheat
Color:	Straw
Price:	$$$

Mike

Nose: A little vanilla and hazelnut with a hint of apples.

Taste: Vanilla, hazelnuts, baking spice, and apples with a hint of oak.

Finish: Medium long with oak and spice.

Susan

Nose: Figs, pepper, and oak.

Taste: Sweet oak with lots of finely ground black pepper.

Finish: Very spicy.

Notes

Top of the Hill Distillery, Chapel Hill, North Carolina. Bottle 425 of Batch 5. Finished with a chip of toasted oak and eight woods total.

My Score

Notes: _____

_____

_____

Appearance (1-5) _____   Nose (1-25) _____

Taste (1-25) _____   Finish (1-25) _____

Complexity (1-10) _____   Overall Impression (1-10) _____

SCORE _____

Woodford Reserve Kentucky Straight Wheat Whiskey

Proof:	90.4
Age:	NAS
Type:	Straight
Style:	Wheat
Mash Bill:	52% wheat, 20% malt, 20% corn, 8% rye
Color:	Straw
Price:	$$$

Mike

Nose: Vanilla, oak, a hint of fruit.

Taste: Vanilla, baking spices, apples, and oak.

Finish: Medium long and spicy.

Susan

Nose: Sweet baking spices, stemmed fruit (fruit cobbler in a glass), with some floral notes.

Taste: Apples, light brown sugar, cinnamon.

Finish: Long and sweet. It's sweet without being cloying.

Notes

Woodford Reserve Distillery, Versailles, Kentucky. With the addition of this to its permanent portfolio, Woodford now offers four styles of American whiskey — bourbon, rye, malt, and wheat.

My Score

Notes: _____

_____

_____

Appearance (1-5) _____   Nose (1-25) _____

Taste (1-25) _____   Finish (1-25) _____

Complexity (1-10) _____   Overall Impression (1-10) _____

SCORE _____

Additional Wheat Whiskey Releases

Name: _____

Distillery: _____

Proof: _____   **Mash Bill:** _____

Age: _____   _____

Type: _____   **Color:** _____

Style: _____   **Price:** _____

My Score

Notes: _____
_____
_____

Appearance (1-5) _____   Nose (1-25) _____

Taste (1-25) _____   Finish (1-25) _____

Complexity (1-10) _____   Overall Impression (1-10) _____

SCORE _____

Name: _____

Distillery: _____

Proof: _____   **Mash Bill:** _____

Age: _____   _____

Type: _____   **Color:** _____

Style: _____   **Price:** _____

My Score

Notes: _____
_____
_____

Appearance (1-5) _____   Nose (1-25) _____

Taste (1-25) _____   Finish (1-25) _____

Complexity (1-10) _____   Overall Impression (1-10) _____

SCORE _____

THE AUTHORS

Susan Reigler
Bourbon Authority and Author

Award-winning writer Susan Reigler was born in Louisville the year Swaps won the Kentucky Derby. From 1992 to 2007, Reigler was a restaurant critic, beverage columnist and travel writer for the Louisville *Courier-Journal.* In addition to *The Bourbon Tasting Notebook* with Michael Veach, she is the author of *Kentucky Bourbon Country: The Essential Travel Guide, The Complete Guide to Kentucky State Parks, The Kentucky Bourbon Cocktail Book, More Kentucky Bourbon Cocktails,* and – coming in spring 2020 – *Which Fork Do I Use with My Bourbon?* co-authored with Peggy Noe Stevens.

With her cat, E.T.

Currently she is a contributing writer to *Bourbon+, American Whiskey Magazine, LEO Weekly* and bourbon columnist for *Food & Dining.* Ms. Reigler is a Certified Executive Bourbon Steward by the Society of the Stave & Thief. She served as the President of the Board of Directors of the Bourbon Women Association from 2015 to 2017.

Among the events at which Ms. Reigler has given presentations are the Kentucky Bourbon Festival, Bourbon & Beyond (Louisville), the Bourbon Women Sip-Osium and bourbon festivals in Chicago, New Orleans, Oxford, MS, Smithfield, VA. She has lead bourbon tastings from Seattle to Savannah as well tastings to benefit non- profit organizations including Locust Grove, The Falls of the Ohio Foundation, and Shaker Village at Pleasant Hill. She has been a judge for numerous bourbon cocktail contests and has helped restaurants and retailers select barrels from Four Roses, Woodford Reserve, Knob Creek, Buffalo Trace, and more for private bourbon bottlings.

Ms. Reigler holds a bachelor's degree in music from Indiana University and a master's degree in zoology from the University of Oxford, which she attended as a Humphrey Scholar.

Michael R. Veach
Bourbon Historian and Author
The Filson Historical Society

Mike Veach is one of the foremost authorities on all things Bourbon, and has spent over 15 years with The Filson Historical Society serving in the role of historian and author. Veach possesses an unsurpassed wealth of knowledge and perspective on an industry that has Kentucky at the forefront of the Bourbon Boom occurring across the United States and abroad.

Mr. Veach is also a recognized author whose articles have been featured in publications such as *The Bourbon Review* and *The Louisville Encyclopedia*. He wrote the foreword for the release of Gerald Carson's *Social History of Bourbon* in 2010, and in 2013 published his own now-widely acclaimed book *Kentucky Bourbon Whiskey: An American Heritage*. He is also co-author of *The Bourbon Tasting Notebook* with Susan Reigler.

Prior to his long tenure at The Filson, Veach spent five years as the North American Archivist for United Distillers. Since then he has also provided research and consulting services for such institutions as the Oscar Getz Museum of Whiskey History, Brown-Forman, Buffalo Trace, Four Roses, and Heaven Hill Distillery.

In 2006, Mike Veach was publicly recognized for his knowledge, activities, and accomplishments surrounding bourbon by being inducted into The Kentucky Bourbon Hall of Fame. He has provided pro-bono services to many major non-profit entities such as The Black Acre Foundation, The Farnsley-Kaufman House, The Farnsley-Moreman Landing, Boy Scouts of America, Girls. Inc in Owensboro and many other organizations including The Filson Historical Society.

Veach holds a BA and MA in History from the University of Louisville. He travels across the country researching, lecturing, and hosting special seminars designed to spread the knowledge of Kentucky Whiskey products and enhance the appreciation of Bourbon. Mr. Veach resides in his hometown of Louisville, KY in the heart of Bourbon Country.

INDICES

Alphabetical
Price
Proof
Special Style
State

ALPHABETICAL

PRICE

Subject to change

$ *($15 and under)*
Calvert Extra • 33
Early Times Kentucky
  Whiskey • 15
Georgia Moon • 60
Henderson Blended American
  Whiskey • 35
Kessler • 36
Mellow Corn • 65
North Fork Rye • 182
Seagram's 7 Crown • 37

$$ *($16 - $25)*
Alibi American Blended
  Whiskey • 32
Ezra Brooks Rye • 141
George Dickel No. 8 • 243
George Dickel No. 12 • 244
George Dickel Rye • 146
George Dickel White Corn
  Whiskey No. 1 • 59
Glen Thunder • 61
Jack Daniel's Old No. 7 • 246
James E. Pepper 1776 Straight
  Rye • 156
Jim Beam Pre-Prohibition Style
  Rye Whiskey • 159
Limestone Branch 100% Malted
  Rye • 169
Old Forester Rye • 184
Old Henry Clay Straight Rye
  Whiskey • 185
Old Overholt Bonded Straight
  Rye Whiskey • 187
Old Overholt Rye • 188
Rebel Yell American Whiskey •
  26
Rittenhouse Bonded Rye • 204
Riverboat Rye • 205
Sam Houston American
  Whiskey • 27
Wild Turkey Rye • 229

$$$ *($26 - $35)*
Bare Knuckle American Wheat
  Whiskey • 251
Bernheim Original Kentucky
  Straight Wheat Whiskey •
  252
Bulleit Rye • 123
The Gentleman American
  Whiskey • 16
Gentleman Jack • 238

George Dickel Cascade
  Hollow • 241
George Remus Rye • 147
Going to the Sun • 79
Gun Fighter American Rye
  Whiskey • 151
High West Double Rye • 153
Jack Daniel's Tennessee Straight
  Rye • 155
James Oliver American
  Whiskey • 18
James Oliver Rye • 157
Jefferson's Rye • 158
Long Road Corn Whiskey • 63
McKenzie Straight Rye • 172
Old 55 Corn Whiskey • 66
O.Z. Tyler Rye • 191
Palmetto Whiskey • 24
Pearse Lyon's Reserve • 87
Sazerac Rye • 212
Still and Oak Straight Rye •
  218
Templeton Rye • 220
Thirteenth Colony Southern
  Rye Whiskey • 221
TOPO Eight Oak Carolina
  Whiskey • 262
Two Med • 93
Virginia Highland Whisky Port
  Cask Finished • 96
Woodford Reserve Kentucky
  Straight Wheat Whiskey •
  263

$$$$ *($36 - $55)*
77 Whiskey Local Rye & Corn •
  110
77 Whiskey New York Wheat •
  250
Alpine Traveler's Rest Single
  Malt • 70
Balcones Baby Blue Corn
  Whiskey • 56
Balcones Texas Rye Whiskey •
  114
Balcones Texas Single Malt •
  71
Bare Knuckle Rye • 115
Basil Hayden's Dark Rye
  Whiskey • 117
Basil Hayden's Rye Whiskey •
  118
Blackback Rye Whiskey • 120

Proof

The following whiskies are considered Barrel Strength/ Cask Strength

SPECIAL STYLE

Barrel Proof

(Also known as Barrel Strength or Cask Strength. No water added before bottling.)

Bad Rock Rye • 113

Balcones Brimstone Corn Whiskey • 57

Balcones Texas Single Malt • 71

Bare Knuckle Single Barrel Rye • 116

Barrell Dovetail • 41

Barrell Whiskey Infinate Barrell • 43

Barrell Whiskey Infinate Barrell Project • 42

Buzzard's Roost Single Barrel Rye • 124

Buzzard's Roost Very Small Batch Straight Rye • 125

Catoctin Creek Roundstone Rye Cask Proof • 129

David James Straight American Whiskey • 14

Dry Fly Wheat Whiskey Cask Strength • 255

Five Fathers Rye • 143

Garryana Native Oak • 77

Ironroot Hubris • 62

Jack Daniel's Single Barrel Select • 245

Kentucky Owl Kentucky Straight Rye • 162

Kings County Empire Rye • 163

Knob Creek Cask Strength Rye • 164

Little Book • 49

MB Roland Corn Whiskey • 64

MB Roland Dark Fired Whiskey • 21

MB Roland Malt • 82

MB Roland Straight Rye • 171

Michter's Barrel Strength Rye • 174

Michter's Single Barrel 25-Year Old Rye • 175

Michter's Toasted Barrel Finished Straight Rye • 176

Old Carter Rye • 183

Parker's Heritage Kentucky Straight Wheat Whiskey • 259

Parker's Heritage Malt • 86

Peerless Oak & Pepper Rye • 192

Peerless Rye Small Batch 2-Year • 193

Peerless Rye Small Batch 3-Year • 194

Peerless Single Barrel • 195

Pikesville Rye • 196

Roaming Man Tennessee Rye • 206

Russell's Reserve Single Barrel Rye • 208

Sagamore Spirit Cask Stength Rye • 209

Single Track Rye • 213

Single Track Spirits Wheat Whiskey • 261

Starlight Indiana Straight Single Barrel Rye 3-Year • 216

Starlight Indiana Straight Single Barrel Rye 4-Year • 217

WhistlePig The Boss Hog • 226

Willett Family Estate Small Batch Rye • 231

Bonded/Bottled-in-Bond

(Whiskey that is at least 4 years old, bottled at 100 proof, and produced by one distiller at one distillery in a single distilling season.)

A.D. Laws Secale Straight Rye Whiskey • 111

Col. E.H. Taylor Straight Rye • 133

Dad's Hat Bonded • 137

George Dickel Bottled-in-Bond • 240

Mellow Corn • 65

New Riff Kentucky Straight Rye • 180

Old Maysville Club Rye • 186

Old Overholt Bonded Straight Rye Whiskey • 187

Outryder • 50

Rittenhouse Bonded Rye • 204

Extra Aged

(10 years and more)

Barrell Dovetail • 41

Bourye • 44

Bulleit 12-Year Rye • 122

David James Straight American Whiskey • 14

Balcones Texas Single Malt • 71

Balcones True Blue Straight Corn Whiskey • 58

Copper Fox Rye • 134

Copper Fox Single Malt • 73

Defiant American Single Malt Whisky • 75

George Washington's Straight Rye • 148

George Washington's Unaged Rye • 149

Limestone Branch 100% Malted Rye • 169

McKenzie Pure Pot Still • 84

O'Danagher's American Hibernian Whiskey • 85

Pearse Lyon's Reserve • 87

Ransom The Emerald 1865 • 25

Single Track Rye • 213

Single Track Spirits Wheat Whiskey • 261

Sonoma County Black Truffle Rye • 214

Sonoma County Cherrywood Rye • 215

Starlight Indiana Straight Single Barrel Rye 3-Year • 216

Starlight Indiana Straight Single Barrel Rye 4-Year • 217

Stonehouse Distillery Rye Whiskey • 219

Straight Triticale Whiskey • 107

Tom's Foolery Rye • 222

Town Branch Rye Whiskey • 223

Woodinville Rye • 233

Single Barrel

(Bottled from a single barrel. Barrel number is usually indicated on the label.)

Bad Rock Rye • 113

Bare Knuckle Single Barrel Rye • 116

Buzzard's Roost Single Barrel Rye • 124

Catoctin Creek Roundstone Rye Cask Proof • 129

Catoctin Creek Roundstone Rye Distiller's Select • 130

Driftless Glen Single Barrel Rye • 140

Greenhat Rye • 150

Highland Laddie Celtic Whiskey • 80

Jack Daniel's Single Barrel Select • 245

Koval Four Grain • 20

Lion's Pride Dark Oat • 104

Lion's Pride Dark Wheat Whiskey • 258

Lion's Pride Organic Rye • 170

Michter's 10-Year Single Barrel Rye • 173

Michter's Single Barrel 25-Year Old Rye • 175

O'Danagher's American Hibernian Whiskey • 85

Peerless Oak & Pepper Rye • 192

Peerless Single Barrel • 195

Russell's Reserve Single Barrel Rye • 208

Starlight Indiana Straight Single Barrel Rye 3-Year • 216

Starlight Indiana Straight Single Barrel Rye 4-Year • 217

Tom's Foolery Rye • 222

Wilderness Trail Settler's Select Rye • 230

Small Batch

(A very fluid, if you will, designation, since it can mean two barrels batched for a bottling or over a hundred. The latter is "small" if a distillery usually batches thousands of barrels.)

Bower Hill Reserve Rye • 121

Bulleit Rye • 123

Buzzard's Roost Very Small Batch Straight Rye • 125

Dad's Hat 90 Proof • 136

Dead Guy Whiskey • 74

Founder's Rye Whiskey • 145

George Dickel Barrel Select • 239

George Remus Rye • 147

Knob Creek Cask Strength Rye • 164

Knob Creek Rye Whiskey • 165

Knob Creek Twice Barreled Rye • 166

Michter's US★1 Sour Mash Whiskey • 23

Michter's US★1 Unblended Small Batch American Whiskey • 22

North Coast Rye • 181

North Fork Rye • 182

Peerless Rye Small Batch 2-Year • 193

STATE

(State of the distillation and/or bottling. If a whiskey is sourced, but not distilled by the company, there is an asterisk (*). It may actually be sourced from the same state. Or not. See each whiskey's entry.)

Additional Releases

Name: _____

Distillery: _____

Proof: _____   **Mash Bill:** _____
Age: _____   _____
Type: _____   **Color:** _____
Style: _____   **Price:** _____

My Score		
Notes: _____		
_____		
_____		
Appearance (1-5) ____	Nose (1-25)	____
Taste (1-25) ____	Finish (1-25)	____
Complexity (1-10) ____	Overall Impression (1-10)	____
SCORE ____		

Name: _____

Distillery: _____

Proof: _____   **Mash Bill:** _____
Age: _____   _____
Type: _____   **Color:** _____
Style: _____   **Price:** _____

My Score		
Notes: _____		
_____		
_____		
Appearance (1-5) ____	Nose (1-25)	____
Taste (1-25) ____	Finish (1-25)	____
Complexity (1-10) ____	Overall Impression (1-10)	____
SCORE ____		

Additional Releases

Name: _____

Distillery: _____

Proof: _____ **Mash Bill:** _____

Age: _____ _____

Type: _____ **Color:** _____

Style: _____ **Price:** _____

My Score

Notes: _____

_____

_____

Appearance (1-5) _____   Nose (1-25) _____

Taste (1-25) _____   Finish (1-25) _____

Complexity (1-10) _____   Overall Impression (1-10) _____

SCORE _____

Name: _____

Distillery: _____

Proof: _____ **Mash Bill:** _____

Age: _____ _____

Type: _____ **Color:** _____

Style: _____ **Price:** _____

My Score

Notes: _____

_____

_____

Appearance (1-5) _____   Nose (1-25) _____

Taste (1-25) _____   Finish (1-25) _____

Complexity (1-10) _____   Overall Impression (1-10) _____

SCORE _____

Additional Releases

Name: _____

Distillery: _____

Proof: _____   **Mash Bill:** _____
Age: _____   _____
Type: _____   **Color:** _____
Style: _____   **Price:** _____

My Score

Notes: _____
_____
_____

Appearance (1-5) ____   Nose (1-25) ____
Taste (1-25) ____   Finish (1-25) ____
Complexity (1-10) ____   Overall Impression (1-10) ____
SCORE ____

Name: _____

Distillery: _____

Proof: _____   **Mash Bill:** _____
Age: _____   _____
Type: _____   **Color:** _____
Style: _____   **Price:** _____

My Score

Notes: _____
_____
_____

Appearance (1-5) ____   Nose (1-25) ____
Taste (1-25) ____   Finish (1-25) ____
Complexity (1-10) ____   Overall Impression (1-10) ____
SCORE ____

Additional Releases

Name: _____

Distillery: _____

Proof: _____ **Mash Bill:** _____

Age: _____ _____

Type: _____ **Color:** _____

Style: _____ **Price:** _____

My Score

Notes: _____
_____
_____

Appearance (1-5) _____ Nose (1-25) _____

Taste (1-25) _____ Finish (1-25) _____

Complexity (1-10) _____ Overall Impression (1-10) _____

SCORE _____

Name: _____

Distillery: _____

Proof: _____ **Mash Bill:** _____

Age: _____ _____

Type: _____ **Color:** _____

Style: _____ **Price:** _____

My Score

Notes: _____
_____
_____

Appearance (1-5) _____ Nose (1-25) _____

Taste (1-25) _____ Finish (1-25) _____

Complexity (1-10) _____ Overall Impression (1-10) _____

SCORE _____

My Top 25 Whiskeys

Name	Total Score	Page #
1. _____	_____	_____
2. _____	_____	_____
3. _____	_____	_____
4. _____	_____	_____
5. _____	_____	_____
6. _____	_____	_____
7. _____	_____	_____
8. _____	_____	_____
9. _____	_____	_____
10. _____	_____	_____
11. _____	_____	_____
12. _____	_____	_____
13. _____	_____	_____
14. _____	_____	_____
15. _____	_____	_____
16. _____	_____	_____
17. _____	_____	_____
18. _____	_____	_____
19. _____	_____	_____
20. _____	_____	_____
21. _____	_____	_____
22. _____	_____	_____
23. _____	_____	_____
24. _____	_____	_____
25. _____	_____	_____

The Bourbon Tasting Notebook, Second Edition
by Susan Reigler and Michael Veach

4" x 8.5", 416 pages, softcover
978-1-942613-93-0 • $19.95

The Bourbon Tasting Notebook, Second Edition is a handy logbook for any bourbon enthusiast. With a record amount of bourbon whiskey aging in warehouses and visits to Kentucky's bourbon distilleries topping half a million annually, it is obvious that bourbon is enjoying unprecedented popularity. This logbook will give bourbon lovers the perfect way to track their samplings, with nearly 350 featured brands.

Bourbon: What the Educated Drinker Should Know
by Tim M. Berra

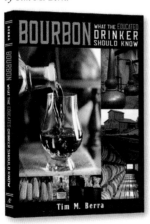

6" x 9", 224 pages, hardcover
978-1-948901-13-0 • $26.95

Oaky and full-bodied, prized throughout the world but distinctly American, with deep roots in the Kentucky hills and hollers… Bourbon has continued to grow as the spirit of choice by alcohol lovers across the globe, but many drinkers have a limited understanding of how bourbon is made. While there may be a hundred books on the subject, few break down the science of bourbon in uncomplicated terms as this lavishly-illustrated book does. A university professor for 50 years, Dr. Tim Berra has developed this authoritative guidebook on all things bourbon in a straightforward, easy to understand format. Berra answers the question "What is Bourbon?" in a style both beginners and aficionados will appreciate, distilling the ba-sics of bourbon into refined sips that are easily consumed.